Overcoming Your Child's Fears and Worries

A Self-help Guide Using Cognitive Behavioral Techniques

Cathy Creswell
Lucy Willetts

EasyRead Large

Copyright Page from the Original Book

Constable & Robinson Ltd
3 The Lanchesters
162 Fulham Palace Road
London W6 9ER
www.constablerobinson.com

First published in the UK by Robinson Publishing Ltd, 2007

This edition published by Robinson,
an imprint of Constable and Robinson Ltd, 2010

Important Note
This book is not intended as a substitute for medical advice or treatment.
Any person with a condition requiring medical attention should consult
a qualified medical practitioner or suitable therapist.

ISBN: 978-1-84529-086-3

Typeset by TW Typesetting, Plymouth, Devon
Printed and bound in the EU

1 3 5 7 9 10 8 6 4 2

TABLE OF CONTENTS

Praise for Overcoming Your Child's Fears and Worries   ii
Acknowledgments   ix
Preface   x
Introduction: Why a cognitive behavioral approach?   xiii

PART ONE: Understanding Your Child's Fears and Worries

    1: What are fears and worries?   3
    2: Common fears and worries experienced by children   8
    3: How do fears and worries develop in children?   25
    4: What keeps children's fears and worries going?   36

PART TWO: Overcoming Your Child's Fears and Worries

    5: A guide to Part Two   47
    6: Step 1: Spotting anxious thinking   59
    7: Step 2: Is that a helpful thought?   71
    8: Step 3: Encouraging independence and 'having a go'   86
    9: Step 4: A step-by-step approach to facing fears   102
    10: Step 5: Problem solving   124
    11: Additional Principles 1: Overcoming worry   139
    12: Additional Principles 2: Managing your own anxiety   151
    13: Some final words on the guide: Keeping it going   169

PART THREE: Addressing Particular Needs

    14: Using this book with younger children   183
    15: Using this book with teenagers   196
    16: Sleep problems   205
    17: Overcoming difficult behavior   218
    18: School refusal   224
    19: Relaxation   236

Appendix 1: Useful resources   247
Appendix 2: Tables   259
Index   265

Cathy Creswell is a clinical psychologist and research fellow at the University of Reading. Since her clinical training, Cathy has worked with children and families in a range of mental health settings such as GP practices, hospitals and a child and adolescent mental health team. She has completed a PhD on the development of anxious thinking styles in children and a diploma in cognitive behavioral therapies for children and adolescents. She has been based at the University of Reading for three years where she conducts research and provides treatment for children with anxiety problems and for their families. She lives in Oxfordshire with her partner, Colin, and son, Joe.

Lucy Willetts is a clinical psychologist who has worked for the NHS in Reading since completing her clinical training 11 years ago. Lucy currently spends part of her time in the Department of Paediatrics at the Royal Berkshire Hospital, working with children with physical health problems. The rest of her time is spent running the Child Anxiety Disorders Research Clinic at the University of Reading, which she set up five years ago. The joint NHS/university clinic offers assessment and treatment to children and adolescents with a range of anxiety problems. Lucy has recently completed a PhD investigating the role of family in the development of childhood anxiety. Lucy lives in Berkshire with her husband, Andrew, and sons, Joslin and Charlie.

Praise for Overcoming Your Child's Fears and Worries

'This excellent book is very well written and is essential reading for any parent who is concerned that their child is anxious. At the outset it provides information to help parents understand the nature of children's fears or concerns, how they develop, and why they persist. It also helps parents to distinguish between what are common and "ordinary" fears and worries, and what kinds of worries might require some form of parental intervention. The book reads very easily and parents would do well to have a copy on their bookshelves to enable them to dip into it at times of stress.'

Alan Stein, Professor of Child and Adolescent Psychiatry, University of Oxford

'I think Cathy Creswell and Lucy Willetts should be congratulated on writing such an accessible yet comprehensive and informative book. They pitch the book at the right level for parents and professionals alike – compassionate and non-judgemental without skimping on the hard facts of the biological, psychological and social realities of these issues. I read it in one sitting and felt I had learnt a lot by the end. I loved the no-nonsense, practical approach that will be an empowering relief to parents, themselves paralysed by the anxiety of their own child's anxieties. Feel a bit jealous that I didn't write it myself!'

Dr Tanya Byron, Consultant Clinical Psychologist, *House of Tiny Tearaways,* **BBC TV**

'This book is a very thorough and detailed practical guide ... which will be very useful for both therapists working with children with fear and worries, as well as families who are able to use this book as a "self-help" treatment guide.'

Dr Penny Titman, Consultant Clinical Psychologist, Great Ormond Street Hospital

'Being frightened and worrying too much of the time gets in the way of children and teenagers playing, having fun together, and getting on with their education. Cathy Creswell and Lucy Willetts have done a great job in making this self-help guide for children, teenagers and parents; explaining in a clear and practical way how therapy is done and how it can be done by families themselves.'

Professor Derek Bolton, Anxiety Clinic for Children and Adolescents, South London and Maudsley NHS Trust

'Learning to live with our children's anxiety is difficult. How do we balance our "instincts" with conflicting advice from different people? How do we know when it's a natural and helpful life experience or when it is less helpful? And how do we know when it's our role as parents to step in? In answering these questions, this book is a breath of fresh air and a godsend for any parent whose child is anxious. Whilst anxiety can be a long-standing problem if untreated, this book instills hope that the right management can help. A sense of collaboration between the authors and the reader, and the parent and their child, is instilled from the word go. It covers everything I would want to see in a book of its kind and more, and helps people to move from a position of powerlessness to the position that something positive can be done.'

Dr Nicky Dummett, Consultant Child and Adolescent Psychiatrist, Leeds and Chair of BABCP Children, Adolescents and Families Special Interest Branch

'This book provides a very helpful framework for supporting parents to adopt a non-judgemental and caring response to problems [such as severe anxiety]. At its centre it asks parents not to assume they know what their child is experiencing and to engage them in respectful and genuinely curious conversations about their difficulties. The book is packed with lots of examples and through these examples the authors clearly convey that their enthusiasm for this approach is tempered by realism, acceptance and an appreciation of the worries and terrors of childhood.'

Dr Peter Fuggle, Consultant Clinical Psychologist, Child and Family Consultation Service, The Northern Health Centre, London

'One of the strengths of this very informative book is the accessibility of the writing style throughout. Even when describing complex concepts the authors do not deviate from this commitment to clarity. There is a refreshing sense of optimism about the work which I would think would increase parental confidence in being involved in tackling their child's anxiety problems. As a clinical psychologist working in a direct access service for parents, I see this book as a most useful resource to be used by the clinician and parent together.'

Yvonne Millar, Consultant Clinical Psychologist, Community Child Psychology Service, The Northern Health Centre, London

And some comments from parents

'After reading your book, which is easy to read and not condescending in any way, we felt that we had some answers, tools and techniques to help our daughter and, frankly, us. As with so many things, once you have the answers, it's so obvious and logical.'

Mr and Mrs W., Oxfordshire

'What a brilliant book! I think that anyone whose child is experiencing anxiety problems will appreciate your suggestions for distractions etc. because it gives you something to do which is positive and then this in turn makes you feel better as a parent. There's no blaming anyone or making you feel inadequate as a parent, just positive steps to take, with good ideas for how to carry them out.'

Mr F., Berkshire

'This is an extremely readable and user-friendly book. The attention to detail and the covering of all bases and eventualities, case studies, tables etc. make the steps in this book as easy as they can be to implement in hectic family life. In addition, the book is very informative and manages to explain what to say to your child in a lot of detail without being at all patronizing. I liked the fact that many of the issues covered in the book would be of benefit to all parents whether their children are anxious or not.'

Mrs C., Berkshire

The aim of the **Overcoming** series is to enable people with a range of common problems and disorders to take control of their own recovery program.

Each title, with its specially tailored program, is devised by a practising clinician using the latest techniques of cognitive behavioral therapy – techniques which have been shown to be highly effective in changing the way patients think about themselves and their problems by changing the way they think about themselves and their difficulties.

The series was initiated in 1993 by Peter Cooper, Professor of Psychology at Reading University in the UK, whose original volume on overcoming bulimia nervosa and binge-eating continues to help many people in the UK, the USA, Australasia and Europe.

Many books in the **Overcoming** series are recommended by the UK Department of Health under the Books on Prescription scheme.

Other titles in the series include:

OVERCOMING ANGER AND IRRITABILITY
OVERCOMING ANOREXIA NERVOSA
OVERCOMING ANXIETY
OVERCOMING BODY IMAGE PROBLEMS INCLUDING
BODY DYSMORPHIC DISORDER
OVERCOMING BULIMIA NERVOSA AND BINGE-EATING
OVERCOMING CHILDHOOD TRAUMA
OVERCOMING CHRONIC FATIGUE
OVERCOMING CHRONIC PAIN
OVERCOMING COMPULSIVE GAMBLING

OVERCOMING DEPERSONALIZATION AND FEELINGS
OF UNREALITY
OVERCOMING DEPRESSION
OVERCOMING GRIEF
OVERCOMING HEALTH ANXIETY
OVERCOMING INSOMNIA AND SLEEP PROBLEMS
OVERCOMING LOW SELF-ESTEEM
OVERCOMING MOOD SWINGS
OVERCOMING OBSESSIVE COMPULSIVE DISORDER
OVERCOMING PANIC AND AGORAPHOBIA
OVERCOMING PARANOID AND SUSPICIOUS THOUGHTS
OVERCOMING PERFECTIONISM
OVERCOMING PROBLEM DRINKING
OVERCOMING RELATIONSHIP PROBLEMS
OVERCOMING SEXUAL PROBLEMS
OVERCOMING SOCIAL ANXIETY AND SHYNESS
OVERCOMING STRESS
OVERCOMING TRAUMATIC STRESS
OVERCOMING WEIGHT PROBLEMS
OVERCOMING WORRY
OVERCOMING YOUR CHILD'S SHYNESS AND SOCIAL
ANXIETY
OVERCOMING YOUR SMOKING HABIT

All titles in the series are available by mail order.

Acknowledgments

We would like to acknowledge the many individuals who have inspired or taught us and have carried out psychological research into anxiety disorders in childhood. The book is not referenced but is heavily influenced by the work of Ron Rapee, Philip Kendall, Paula Barrett, Vanessa Cobham, Lynne Murray, Peter Cooper and our colleagues at the Winnicott Research Unit. We would like to thank Sarah Cook, Kim Freeman, Liesbeth Teagle and Sue Pitt for the time they have spent and all their extremely helpful and encouraging feedback on an earlier draft of this book. Our appreciation also goes to Sandra Rigby and Fritha Saunders of Constable and Robinson, and particularly Peter Cooper, who has no doubt gone above and beyond his editorial role in helping us to make this book happen. To our families, Colin and Joe, and Andrew, Joslin and Charlie, we thank you for your patience and understanding (and general picking up of the pieces). Finally, and most of all, we would like to thank all the families we have worked with and from whom we have learned so much.

Preface

Having a child who is anxious is extremely worrying. And, as if seeing your child in an anxious state wasn't enough, on top of that is the confusion of trying to decide between your own instincts and all the different advice that other people will have given you in an attempt to help: 'Just ignore him', 'Just make her do it', 'Don't give in to him'.

Lucy and I are both child clinical psychologists who have completed doctoral research on the development of anxiety in children. We currently run the Child Anxiety Disorders Research Clinic, a joint project between Berkshire Healthcare Trust and the University of Reading, one of the few specialist centres for the treatment of anxiety disorders in children in the UK. Between us, Lucy and I have worked with hundreds of families in which children have significant problems with fears and worries and, despite each family having its own unique story, we are repeatedly struck by the similarities that they share. One is the uncertainty about how best to help their child move forward whilst preventing him or her becoming continually distressed. Another is a set of natural patterns that evolve within families in response to trying to carry on with life in this context. Your child's fears and worries may have started to define your lives, in determining where you can or can't go or what you can or can't do, or you may be concerned that this is the way things may be heading.

In writing this book, Lucy and I are extremely conscious that a great many of the parents we work with come to us with concerns that they may have somehow caused their child's problem or made it worse in some way. In Part One of this book we will describe some of the potential causes of child anxiety. For now though we would like to emphasize that it is extremely unlikely that there will ever be one single cause. Rather it is likely to be a wealth of different factors that have interacted to bring about the situation that your child is currently in. While anxious children, and often their families too, can easily get into vicious cycles in which their attempts to make things easier in the short term can lead to problems continuing in the long term, it is our experience that what parents have done along the way, they have done because it seemed like the best thing to do for their child at that time and a better alternative just wasn't apparent.

Throughout this book we will be talking you through sets of principles to help you identify the patterns or vicious cycles that you and/or your child may have got stuck in and equipping you with additional skills and strategies either to break these cycles or prevent them from occurring. Our aim is to put you and your child back in control of your lives. The step-by-step program that we describe is based on tried and tested treatment strategies developed in various major research centres around the world in combination with our experiences of what works for young people and their families. Along the way you will read other parents' experiences of living with an anxious child and their ways of overcoming their fears and worries. These stories are based on real families that we have worked with; however, names and details have been changed to prevent identification.

The amount of time that it takes to make changes to your child's fears and worries is highly variable, depending on a number of factors, including the length of time the fear or worry has been a problem and how specific a fear it is. It is important to realize that changes won't all happen overnight and that progress may not follow a straight path; to bring about change will take time, effort, patience and perseverance. Nonetheless, research has shown that if the principles described here are followed, significant gains can be made. We wish you all the best with your efforts.

Cathy Creswell

Introduction: Why a cognitive behavioral approach?

The approach this book takes in attempting to help you overcome your child's fears and worries is a cognitive behavioral one. You might find this brief account of the history of this form of treatment helpful and encouraging. In the 1950s and 1960s a set of therapeutic techniques was developed, collectively termed 'behavior therapy'. These techniques shared two basic features. First, they aimed to remove symptoms (such as anxiety) by dealing with those symptoms themselves, rather than their deep-seated underlying historical causes (traditionally the focus of psychoanalysis, the approach developed by Sigmund Freud and his associates). Second, they were techniques loosely related to what laboratory psychologists were finding out about the mechanisms of learning, which could potentially be put to the test, or had already been proven to be of practical value to sufferers. The area where these techniques proved to be of most value was in the treatment of anxiety disorders, especially specific phobias (such as extreme fear of animals or heights) and agoraphobia, all notoriously difficult to treat using conventional psychotherapies.

After an initial flush of enthusiasm, discontent with behavior therapy grew. There were a number of reasons for this, an important one of which was the fact that behavior therapy did not deal with the internal thoughts which were so obviously central to the distress that many patients were experiencing. In particular, behavior therapy proved inadequate when it came to the treatment of depression. In the late 1960s and early 1970s, a treatment for depression was developed called 'cognitive therapy'. The pioneer in this enterprise was an American psychiatrist, Professor Aaron T. Beck. He developed a theory of depression that emphasized the importance of people's depressed styles of thinking, and on the basis of this theory, he specified a new form of therapy. It would not be an exaggeration to say that Beck's work has changed the nature of psychotherapy, not just for depression but for a range of psychological problems.

The techniques introduced by Beck have been merged with the techniques developed earlier by the behavior therapists to produce a therapeutic approach that has come to be known as 'cognitive behavioral therapy' (or CBT). This therapy has been subjected to the strictest scientific testing and it has been found to be a highly successful treatment for a significant proportion of cases of depression. It has now become clear that specific patterns of disturbed thinking are associated with a wide range of psychological problems, not just depression, and that the treatments which deal with these are highly effective. So effective cognitive behavioral treatments have been developed for anxiety disorders like panic disorder, generalized anxiety disorder, specific phobias, social phobia, obsessive compulsive disorders, and hypochondriasis (health anxiety), as well as for other conditions such as compulsive gambling, drug addiction, and eating disorders like bulimia nervosa. Indeed, cognitive behavioral techniques have been found to have an application beyond the narrow categories of psychological disorders. They have been applied effectively, for example, to help people with low self-esteem, people with weight problems, couples with marital difficulties, as well as those who wish to give up smoking or deal with drinking problems.

The starting point for CBT is the realization that the ways we think, feel and behave are all intimately linked, and changing the way we think about ourselves, our experiences, and the world around us, changes the way we feel and what we are able to do. So, for example, by helping a depressed person identify and challenge their automatic depressive thoughts, a route out of the cycle of depressive thoughts and feelings can be found. Similarly, habitual behavioral responses are driven by a complex set of thoughts and feelings, and CBT, as you will discover from this book, by providing a means for the behavior to be brought under cognitive control, enables these responses to be undermined and a different kind of life to be possible.

In recent years, CBT treatments have been developed for children and adolescents and the research has produced very encouraging results, especially for the treatment of children's anxiety problems. Often these treatments involve clinicians working with both the child and the child's parent(s), although working with parents alone to help them help their child has in some studies been found to be just as effective.

Although effective CBT treatments have been developed for a wide range of disorders and problems, these treatments are not widely available and when people try on their own to help themselves or their children, they often, inadvertently, do things that make matters worse. In recent years the community of cognitive behavioral therapists has responded to this situation by taking the principles and techniques of specific cognitive behavioral therapies for particular problems and presenting them in manuals that people can read and apply. These manuals specify a systematic program of treatment, which the person works through to overcome their difficulties. In this way, cognitive behavioral therapeutic techniques of proven value are being made available on the widest possible basis. This manual has been written specifically for parents of children with excessive and troubling fears and worries and it provides them with a clear set of therapeutic principles that they can systematically apply to help their children.

Self-help manuals are never going to replace therapists. Many families will need treatment from a qualified therapist. It is also the case that, despite the widespread success of cognitive behavioral therapy, some people will not respond to it and will need one of the other treatments available. Nevertheless, although research on the use of these self-help manuals is at an early stage, the work done to date indicates that for a great many people such a manual is sufficient for them to overcome their problems without professional help. Many families suffer on their own for years. Sometimes they feel reluctant to seek help without first making a serious effort to manage on their own. Sometimes appropriate help is not forthcoming despite their efforts to find it. For many of these families the cognitive behavioral self-help manual will provide a lifeline to recovery and a better future.

Peter J. Cooper
The University of Reading

PART ONE

Understanding Your Child's Fears and Worries

1

What are fears and worries?

Although it may be tempting to skip this section and get stuck straight into working on changing things, we want to encourage you strongly to take the time to read through these first four brief chapters before you start to read Part Two. There are three main reasons for this. Firstly, Chapters 1 and 2 describe the problem of fears and worries in children. By reading them you will be able to make sure that this is the right book for you, in the sense that it is focused on the problem that you want to work on with your child (or encourage someone else to work on with their child). Secondly, Chapters 3 and 4 explain how fears and worries develop in young people and what keeps these fears and worries going. The information given in these chapters provides the rationale for all the work you will do when you follow the guide in Part Two. Having a clear understanding of why you are doing what you are doing will make it much easier for you to put the strategies into place and will encourage you to persevere when the going is tough. Thirdly, in Part One you will be introduced to four children: Ben, Tom, Jenny and Sarah. These children have all experienced fears and worries, and in Part One you will hear some of the background to

4

their difficulties, before reading in Part Two about how their parents helped them to overcome these.

We appreciate that you will be keen to get going with the central theme of the book – the actual overcoming of fears and worries – and we have therefore kept Part One brief. Please do read on.

What do we mean by fears and worries?

Everyone, children and adults alike, experiences worries, fears and anxiety some of the time. What worries, fears and anxiety have in common is that they involve an expectation that something bad is going to happen, a particular way in which our bodies respond to this and certain characteristic behaviors.

Anxious thinking

When people become anxious most commonly they will be thinking that 'something bad' is about to happen. At this time thoughts tend to become focused on the potential threat and how to escape from it, and it can be hard to think about anything else. This is clearly a useful state to be in when someone is in danger. For example, if your child is about to step into the road you need to be focused on getting your child out of the way of oncoming traffic and not be easily distracted by other thoughts, such as what you need to buy at the shops or what you are having for dinner.

Bodily changes

When we experience fears and worries, we respond in a number of ways. These include our breathing getting faster, heart rate speeding up, muscles becoming tense, sweating and 'butterflies' in the tummy. All of these bodily signs represent our body getting ready for action, enabling us to react quickly and, as in the above example, pulling the child out of the way before he or she comes to any harm.

Anxious behavior

The way we behave in response to fears or worries can generally be categorized as either a 'fight' or 'flight' response: we either fight against the threat or we get out of the way as quickly as we can. Once again, when we are faced with immediate threats these are, of course, the most helpful ways to respond.

As we can see, the feelings that we have described above are not necessarily bad for us. In fact they can help us to perform well – for example, by motivating us to prepare before a big test or to 'psych us up' before a performance. Sometimes they can be essential for our survival.

So if it's normal to be anxious, why am I so concerned about my child?

The changes that we experience in response to anxiety are helpful in the short term, but if these reactions continue to occur when actual danger has passed, or when, in fact, it was never there, they become problematic. Over time the bodily changes can become very uncomfortable. Children who are highly anxious often complain of tummy aches, headaches or muscle aches. When anxiety is excessive, thinking can become dominated by fearing the worst: your child may always seem to expect the worst to happen and lack confidence in his or her ability to cope with any challenge. Finally, when anxiety persists, not only is it exhausting to feel constantly 'on edge' but also trying to keep away from potential danger can lead your child to miss out on doing things that he or she would otherwise enjoy. If fears and worries are getting in the way of your child enjoying him- or herself and being able to do the things that other children of the same age are doing, then it is important that he or she is helped to overcome these difficulties. This book is about giving you the tools to help your child to do just that.

As we have seen, a certain amount of fear and worry is both normal and healthy, so the aim of this book is not to help you to get your child to a point where he or she *never* worries or is *never* scared. Instead, our aim is to assist you in helping your child take control of his or her fears and worries so that they do not get in the way of him or her getting the most out of life.

When children with anxiety problems receive appropriate treatment, they generally do very well. There is a lot of information in this book, but the central message is simple: anxiety problems are extremely common among children, they can present a serious problem, and they *can* be overcome.

2

Common fears and worries experienced by children

All children will experience fears and worries differently, and while using this book it is important for you to try to get a thoroughly clear understanding of your child's unique experience. Every family we work with describes an experience that we have not heard about before. However, they also have a great deal in common with other families. The basic patterns of anxious thinking, behavior and physical symptoms have been described in Chapter 1; however, we can also group certain types of anxiety problems together based on more specific features or symptoms. These groups of anxiety problems have been given labels called 'diagnoses'. The most common categories of anxiety problems among children are: specific phobias, social phobia, generalized anxiety, separation anxiety, panic disorder, obsessive compulsive disorder (OCD) and post-traumatic stress disorder (PTSD). What is meant by each of these categories will be described below.

Specific phobias

When a fear of a particular place, object or situation becomes a problem it is called a phobia. Specifically this describes a fear that is excessive and leads to avoidance or extreme discomfort when a child is faced with the feared object (or place or situation). Fears are common; for example, a lot of people are cautious of spiders, snakes or bees and this can be a healthy response. If, however, your child's fear is significantly interfering with his or her life, such as causing problems at school, in the family or with friends, or if it stops him or her from doing things he or she would like to do, then it would no doubt be best for your child to receive help in overcoming this fear.

The feared object that drives a phobia can be anything, and this is clearly demonstrated by lists of weird and wonderful phobia names that include over 500 different types of phobias. Some of the most common phobias are: spiders (arachnophobia), bees (apiphobia), wasps (spheksophobia), thunder and lightning (brontophobia), blood (haematophobia), water (hydrophobia), birds (ornithophobia), dogs (cynophobia), other animals (zoo-phobia), vomit (emotophobia), choking (pnigophobia), and fear of leaving a place of safety (agoraphobia).

Sarah (aged 10)

Sarah has never liked spiders. I remember when she was just a toddler she once became hysterical because she saw a bit of fluff on the carpet which looked a bit like a spider. Since then she has always had to keep away if we came across a spider in the room but it never used to cause a big problem. Over time it just seems to have got worse. Now we're finding that there are certain places that Sarah won't want to go to because she thinks we're likely to see a spider. For example, her granddad had to go into hospital for a month so his flat was empty for all that time. We went over to give it a clean up before he came home. We shouldn't have taken Sarah with us really because, not surprisingly, we came across a spider before too long. Sarah got really upset and was out the door before you could do anything about it. Since then she has refused to go back to her granddad's house so he always has to come to us to visit, which feels unfair on him.

Social phobia

Social phobias are different from the very specific phobias that we have described above, because the child can fear a variety of different situations. What these situations have in common, however, is that the child fears that he or she will do something that he or she will be embarrassed or ashamed by. For children this can make it difficult to enter into situations where there will be other people – for example, going to school, being with other children (such as at parties), and going to restaurants. Although children with social phobia may be perfectly comfortable when they are with people they know well, they may try to avoid situations where there will be less familiar people or may feel very uncomfortable if they have to be in these kinds of situations. (For more specific advice on dealing with this problem see *Overcoming Your Child's Shyness and Social Anxiety* by Lucy Willetts and Cathy Creswell.)

Jenny (aged 11)

Jenny's biggest problem is with school. In the summer holidays she's like a different person. Then maybe a week before she's due to go back she'll start getting the tummy aches. It's the same on a Sunday evening during the school term. It's really hard to know if she is genuinely ill or not, especially as sometimes she is physically sick and she tends to go white as a sheet at the mention of going to school. This problem has been around for a while although in year 6 she had a really supportive teacher and things seemed to settle down for a bit. Since she's been at secondary school though she's found it really hard. She seems to think everybody thinks badly of her. So any little thing will upset her, like if another child is just looking at her she'll think they are thinking there is something wrong with her hair or her clothes. Her teachers have told me that she is really quiet in class and never puts her hand up or tries to participate. She often comes home with no idea of what she should be doing for her homework as she hasn't understood it but hasn't asked the teacher what to do.

Generalized anxiety

The term generalized anxiety describes a situation where a child worries excessively and finds it hard to get worries out of his or her mind. The worries tend to be about a range of different concerns, rather than a single issue; for example, common worries can include things going on in the world (such as terrorism or epidemics), getting things right and the health of ourselves and others. The worries are often accompanied by unpleasant physical symptoms such as difficulty concentrating, muscle aches, sleep problems (difficulty settling or frequent waking), irritability and tiredness. Again, these difficulties can interfere with the child's ability to enjoy activities at home, school, in the family or with friends.

Ben (aged 7)

The best way to describe Ben is as 'a worrier'. He seems to worry about anything and everything. I have stopped putting the news on when he is around because it's like he is on the lookout for bad news. For example, he is terrified that we are all going to catch Bird Flu. He also gets really wound up when his Dad has to go into the city for work as he has seen stories about bombs and terrorism. I suppose I can understand those worries, but there are others I find harder. He just gets something into his head and it seems to get stuck there. Like he has a real worry about this creature called 'Drog' that was in a film that he watched at his cousin's house. He is convinced that if he goes upstairs Drog is going to come and get him, to the point that he won't go upstairs on his own. We tell him that there is no Drog and just to forget about it but he just can't seem to get rid of this thought. Since this has been going on he has had to share a bedroom with his brother, but it takes Ben so long to get to sleep at night because he is worrying about something or other that this is now disturbing his brother's sleep too.

Separation anxiety

Some children find it extremely difficult to be apart from a parent or other carer. This often relates to a fear that if they are separated from the carer they will not see each other again. This can either be because of a fear that some harm will come to the child if the carer is not present (such as they will get taken or injured), or that harm will come to the carer in the child's absence. These fears make it difficult for a child to take part in a range of activities that other children of the same age will be doing, including attending school, visiting friends, going to after-school clubs or activities, or going to sleep independently of the carer.

Tom (aged 9)

There are a lot of things Tom finds difficult, but I think the one I struggle with the most is bedtime. Tom needs to have me or my partner there with him for him to go to sleep. We feel like we have tried everything – we have insisted he stay in his room and have let him cry, but he just got himself so worked up that it seemed to make things worse; we decorated his room for him so that it would be a nice place to be – none of these things have made any difference. What tends to happen is that one of us will go in with Tom and read him a story and then we have to lie down on his bed with him until he drops off. Quite often we'll end up dropping off, too, then we lose a big chunk of our evening. Then when we finally do get to bed, more often than not we'll be woken up to find Tom has crept in, too, at some point in the night. I think the fact that none of us are getting enough sleep is making everything else harder to deal with. The other big thing is, of course, school. Tom has missed a great deal of school this year as he just finds it so difficult, and we just don't have the energy to keep pushing him to going anymore. It just doesn't seem like it can be good for him to go through so much stress each day. I try to imagine him ten years from now. He certainly can't be coming in to our bed then. Something has to be done.

Panic disorder

A 'panic attack' is an intense feeling of anxiety accompanied by striking physical symptoms, such as difficulty breathing, chest pains, sweating, hot (or cold) flushes and tingling, or 'pins and needles'. Panic attacks typically come on very quickly, especially if a person is taking rapid, short breaths, as these exacerbate many of the other symptoms. Panic often occurs alongside other types of anxiety difficulties. It can be triggered by the child entering into a particular feared situation and feeling unable to cope. It can also be set off by a physical sensation – for example, if a person feels chest pain (perhaps from indigestion) or feels dizzy (such as from overexertion) and interprets this as a sign of serious illness.

Jenny (aged 11)

The first time Jenny had a panic attack it scared the life out of me. We were just about to leave the house. Everything had seemed normal. Then suddenly she had her hand on her chest as if she was about to keel over and it was if she couldn't breathe – she was really struggling to catch her breath. I tried to take hold of her hand and I felt it was really hot and sweaty. I didn't know what to do. I kept telling her to slow down and to try to take deep breaths, but it was as if she couldn't hear what I was saying. I had to call an ambulance because I thought there was something seriously wrong with her – like something wrong with her heart. When the ambulance came they said it was a panic attack and showed her how to take slow, deep breaths, which seemed to help her calm down. They asked if there was anything that was worrying Jenny and she said that there wasn't, but when I spoke to her teacher later I found out that Jenny's class were due to do a class assembly that day. I guess all the worry had just got too much for her. The trouble is I think she is now worried not only about all the school issues but also about having another one of these attacks, which is making it even harder for her to do any of the things that make her nervous.

Other anxiety disorders

Part Two of this book is principally focused upon helping children to overcome the anxiety problems described above. Two other major types of anxiety problems are OCD and PTSD. Below we will briefly describe the difficulties associated with these disorders. As far as OCD and PTSD are concerned, however, treatment approaches that are applied in clinics have some crucial differences from the approach taken in this book. Using the strategies described in this book will certainly not do your child any harm, but if your child is experiencing problems relating to OCD or PTSD we would recommend you seek more specific advice and support (see listings in Appendix 1, Useful Resources).

Obsessive Compulsive Disorder (OCD)

OCD is characterized by the experience of intrusive thoughts or images (obsessions) and a compulsion to act in a particular way in response to these thoughts. The thoughts or images typically seem just to pop into a child's mind, causing distress. These obsessions occur frequently and are unwanted, and a child will find it difficult to control or get rid of them. Obsessions differ from real-life worries or concerns, as they often take the form of a specific concern that the child feels responsible for prevents (for example, my mother will die unless I tell her I love her six times a day). Common obsessions in OCD include fears about contamination, doubts about harm occurring (such as door locks not being secure) and excessive concern with exactness or symmetry. Compulsions are behaviors that a child repeats over and over again to try to avoid harm or to make him- or herself feel more comfortable. These can be things a child does in his or her mind (such as counting or saying special words over and over) or something observable by others (such as checking locks or switches, washing or ordering things). Mild forms of this phenomenon are very common in childhood and are not a cause for concern. However, when symptoms of OCD are interfering with the child's life, early recognition and treatment lead to a better outcome for the child, so in these cases it is important to seek help from your general practitioner. Additional resources are also listed in Appendix 1.

Post-Traumatic Stress Disorder (PTSD)

PTSD describes a reaction to a traumatic event in which a child directly experienced or witnessed the threat of actual or perceived death or injury to the child or another person. At the time the child would have felt fear, helplessness or horror, and this is followed by recurrent, vivid memories or dreams of the event, avoidance of reminders of the event, and/or increased sensitivity to fear. This reaction reflects a natural process of recovery after a traumatic experience; however, in some cases symptoms persist. If symptoms continue for more than a month it is advisable to seek support via your general practitioner. Additional resources are listed in Appendix 1.

How common are fears and worries in children?

Anxiety problems are the most common form of emotional and behavioral problems experienced by young people. Studies have estimated that between 5 and 10 per cent of children meet criteria for a diagnosis of anxiety disorder. In other words, at least one in every 20 children is likely to have a significant anxiety problem, and it could be as many as one in ten. The table over the page represents the average frequencies of the specific types of anxiety problem that we have discussed. These figures are averages based on children and adolescents, but certain difficulties are more common at different ages. Specifically, separation anxiety disorder is more commonly found among pre-adolescent children than adolescents; and social phobia and panic disorder are more common among adolescent than pre-adolescent children. In adolescence we also find a greater number of girls than boys who are experiencing anxiety disorders, which may be accounted for by the fact that more girls than boys tend to experience problems with both panic and social phobia at this age.

TABLE 2.1: THE PREVALENCE OF ANXIETY DISORDERS AMONG CHILDREN IN THE GENERAL COMMUNITY

Anxiety disorder	Prevalence in the general community
Specific phobias	3 per cent
Social phobia	1 per cent
Generalized anxiety disorder	2 per cent

Anxiety disorder	Prevalence in the general community
Separation anxiety disorder	3 per cent
Panic disorder	0.2 per cent
OCD	1 per cent
PTSD	unknown

From F.C. Verhulst, 'Community and epidemiological aspects of anxiety disorders in children', in W.K. Silverman and P.D.A. Treffers, Anxiety Disorders in Children and Adolescents: Research, Assessment and Intervention, Cambridge University Press (2001).

The effects on children's lives

The effects on social life

Tom (aged 9)

Tom is at an age now where all his friends are starting to sleep over at each other's houses and go away to camps and things like that. We've tried to get Tom along to an after-school football club but he'll only join in if he knows he will be able to see me throughout. He has a 'school journey' coming up next term and I think there is no way he will be able to go. I feel like he is really missing out and I worry that his friends are going to lose interest as he gets older if Mum or Dad are always hanging about.

It is easy to see how certain anxiety problems can affect children's developing social lives. Throughout childhood friendships are essential for children to learn and practise what they need to know to form lasting relationships. They also provide an essential reference point by which children can discover that many of the challenges they experience are quite normal. Friends also, of course, provide opportunities for fun, and encourage and motivate each other to try new experiences. Throughout childhood and adolescence relationships between friends are constantly changing. When anxiety causes a child to withdraw from school or other social opportunities a vicious cycle can become established, because changes that have occurred within his or her group of friends make it harder for the child to join it again, as shown in the diagram below.

The effects on academic performance

There is no reason to think that children who have problems with anxiety are, on the whole, any less bright than children who do not have anxiety problems. Despite this, children with anxiety problems do tend to experience more academic problems. This is likely to be because their anxiety is preventing them from achieving their full potential.

Figure 2.1 Cycle created when a child misses school

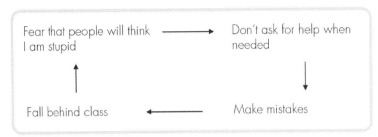

Figure 2.2 Cycle created when a child is anxious about seeking help at school

Jenny (aged 11)

Jenny is now having a real problem at school. The fact that she misses more days from school than most children because she makes herself so ill isn't a good start. She has always struggled a bit with her work but it is just getting worse and worse now, as she isn't getting the help she needs because she never lets the teacher know that she needs it.

Again, a vicious cycle can develop with regard to children's academic achievements, in which missed days at school, or difficulties accessing help, lead to problems with school, which in turn leads to greater anxiety about one's ability to get the work done, as shown in the diagram above.

The effects on mood

About half of all children who experience significant anxiety problems also experience symptoms of low mood or depression, such as loss of interest in their usual activities, tearfulness or irritability, feelings of worthlessness, and physical symptoms such as poor appetite and sleep problems. All children (and adults for that matter) feel down from time to time, but if these kinds of feelings are continuous (say for a period of two weeks or more), and it seems impossible to lift your child out of this low mood then your child may be depressed.

Ben (aged 7)

Ben just seems to have the weight of the world on his shoulders. It seems like such a rare occurrence that I see him laugh or smile. It makes me really sad to think that such a young boy feels that way. Other children his age seem to be laughing and joking without a care. I just wish he could be the same way.

The strategies that are described in Part Two of this book are useful skills for life and can be helpful for overcoming mild to moderate levels of depression. If your child falls into this category, you may find that by helping him or her to overcome his or her fears or worries he or she will begin to feel better about him- or herself and be more able to participate in activities that he or she will find fulfilling. However, if your child is extremely withdrawn and lacking in motivation, you may find it difficult to apply many of the strategies that we will introduce you to. In this case we would recommend you visit your general practitioner to discuss ways that you and your child could access greater support to help improve his or her mood before embarking on this program.

Will my child grow out of this problem?

Studies that have kept in touch with children with anxiety disorders over time have tended to report that spontaneous recovery (that is, getting better without treatment) is generally slow, and that symptoms typically persist for several years. When we consider the effects that anxiety problems can have on children's social lives, academic performance and mood, this presents a gloomy picture. On the other hand it is important to stress that treatments for childhood anxiety have excellent success rates. The clear implication of this is that if your child is experiencing anxiety problems then it is important that this is recognized and dealt with.

3

How do fears and worries develop in children?

Ben (aged 7)

Ben has always been a worrier. He always seems to see and fear the worst happening. I see other children his age and these kinds of thoughts don't even seem to cross their minds. I do think a lot about what must have caused it. On the one hand it seems like he has always been a bit this way. Even when he was a baby he seemed jumpy and found it really hard to relax. It was always a real job to get him to sleep at night. There are other people who worry a lot in my family so I guess that must be a part of it. He has also had a lot to cope with in his life so far. He lost two grandparents whom he was very close to within a year and that was very upsetting for him. I also can't help thinking, 'Is it something that we've done?', 'Have we made him this way somehow?'

The majority of parents whom we have worked with who have children with anxiety problems have been keen to get a better understanding of why their child has fears and worries. This is partly to enable them to help their child overcome these fears and worries, but it is sometimes also because parents worry that they are in some way to blame for their child's anxiety. Parents certainly can influence how anxious their child becomes in particular situations (and if they couldn't there would be no point to a book like this!). It is rare, however, for a child's fears and worries to be caused by just one thing. A child's anxiety level and the extent that this interferes with his or her life are, instead, generally a result of a variety of influences. This chapter will talk you through the most common factors: (i) genetics and inherited personality characteristics; and (ii) learning experiences, including what is learned from other people and specific life events.

What do we inherit?

It is well known that we all inherit certain physical characteristics from our parents; for example, eye colour, hair colour, stature and a range of other physical features. The same is true for psychological characteristics. We can inherit a tendency to have a quick temper, be impulsive, or be laid back. You are likely to feel that many of the ways your child responds to things (emotionally or behaviorally) resemble how you or other people in your family also respond (or might have responded when you were children).

It is now also well known that 'anxiety runs in families'. Studies that have assessed family members of children who are anxious have tended to find higher rates of anxiety in parents and siblings than would be explained by chance. In general, research has suggested that there is a clear genetic influence on anxiety in childhood. Although estimates vary across studies, about one-third of the influence on general anxiety seems to be caused by genetics. In other words, anxiety is caused by one part genes and two parts experiences.

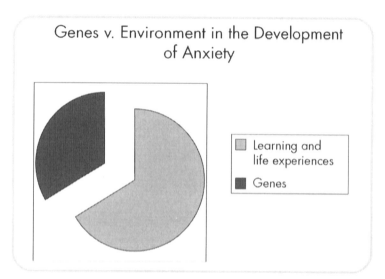

Figure 3.1 Pie chart showing contribution of genes and life experiences towards anxiety

Genes v. environment in the development of anxiety

What exactly is inherited?

Although a boy and his father may both be great football players, we wouldn't normally think that this means football playing ability is 'in their genes'. It is quite likely, however, that other characteristics which help someone to be good at football (such as strength, speed and quick reactions) may at least be partly inherited. It is probable that anxiety runs in families for similar reasons. Rather than us inheriting a particular anxiety disorder, we are likely to inherit certain characteristics that make us more inclined to become highly anxious at some point in our lives. Two candidates for what is inherited are (i) how easily our body jumps to action in response to threat (such as how easily a baby is startled by loud noises), and (ii) how generally emotional we are (such as how easily a baby becomes distressed).

The environmental element

At this point you may well be thinking 'If my child was born this way then what hope do I have of changing it?' This is a common reaction; however, as we have seen, genetics can never fully tell us whether a child is going to develop problems with fears or anxiety. There are a large number of children who may come from a family of 'worriers' but who never experience excessive fear or worry themselves. Similarly, your child may have brothers or sisters who do not appear anxious in the least. There are also many children who may have seemed easily upset as babies, difficult to settle and reserved as toddlers but who go on to experience no problems with fears or worries. Indeed, when it comes to anxiety problems the contribution of genetics to the cause is modest and does not mean that the child's environment and life experiences won't make a difference to his or her development. Clearly the experiences that the child has in his or her life have a crucial influence on how fears and worries develop.

Adverse life events

Tom (aged 9)

I don't feel that Tom has had the best start in life. There has been so much upheaval. I split up from his birth dad when he was just a baby and he hasn't really had any consistent contact with him throughout his life. I've been with my partner for most of Tom's life, and Tom thinks of him as 'Dad', but he has a job that involves him being away a lot of the time. We have also had to move quite a lot for various reasons, including financial problems, so there has been quite a bit of stress in the family, and Tom has changed schools and moved away from his old friends. I guess if I was him maybe I'd be anxious, too.

As we have said above, many parents report that their child has always seemed to be fearful or a worrier. But they also often say that the fears or worries got worse or began to cause more disruption after a major life event. It is difficult to know for sure whether people who experience a lot of fears and worries have had more stressful events happen in their lives or not. The reason for this is that a stressful event may have a much bigger impact on an anxious person than the same event would have on a less anxious person. Equally, however, for some children difficult experiences can sometimes have a 'toughening up' effect. You may be able to think of two children you know who have had similar difficult life experiences but have responded to them in completely different ways. It seems that the influence of stressful experiences on children's fears and worries depends on factors other than the nature of the experience alone. This can include the child's genetic vulnerability to anxiety, but also other environmental influences such as what the child learns from the people around him or her.

LEARNING BY EXAMPLE

From a young age children learn from watching other people around them. When toddlers enter a new situation they will be learning how to respond by watching those around them. Children are likely to rely most heavily on information they get from watching those who are close to them, such as parents, or carers, and siblings. In order to survive in the world it is essential that children learn in this way, to help them to stay away from potential danger and harm. This process has very clear advantages. The disadvantage is that children can learn unhelpful responses from those close to them, too.

Jenny (aged 11)

I am doing my best to help Jenny get over her fears but I know I don't always set a very good example. For example, when I used to go with her to the school gates I used to find it really difficult. There are so many other parents there. They all seem to know each other. In that situation I find I just tend to try and keep my head down and get in and out as quickly as I can.

Parents are often aware of their own fears and worries and make a conscious effort to cover them up from their children for exactly this reason. Children are highly tuned to their carers' reactions, however, and can be extremely good at picking up subtle signs that something is wrong. For example, Joe (who is discussed in Chapter 14 on working with younger children) is scared of dogs. His dad isn't keen on dogs either but makes an effort to hide this fear from Joe. If Joe's dad is walking down the street with Joe and he sees a big dog coming towards them he will contain his fear and calmly cross the road so that he is not put in a situation in which Joe will see him get scared. Nonetheless, from the fact that they have crossed the road Joe has picked up a message from his dad that there is good reason to stay away from dogs.

LEARNING FROM OTHER PEOPLE'S REACTIONS

As well as watching what other people do, children are also on the lookout for how other people react to what they do. Parents may encourage their child to avoid situations that they fear.

Ben (aged 7)

What would I do if Ben asked to go up to London for his birthday? I think I'd fall off my chair! Well, no, I guess I'd be really pleased that he wanted to do that. But I'd be pretty doubtful that he'd make it. He might say he wants to but as the time approaches he would start to worry about it and it would end up just ruining his birthday. I think all I could do really was try to suggest other things when he brought it up – maybe do something local where we don't need to go on public transport or do anything he might see as dangerous.

Similarly, if a child does enter into a potentially difficult situation, parents may, inadvertently, respond in a way that increases the child's fear. For example, when Joe strokes a dog, does his dad smile and look comfortable, or does he look concerned, serious or uncomfortable? When Jenny reads a line in a school assembly, does her mum sit nodding and looking relaxed and confident in Jenny's ability, or does she sit on the edge of her chair, wringing her hands, worrying how Jenny is going to get on? As we have described above, many anxious children do seem fearful early in their lives and/or they may have had some difficult experiences to cope with. It is not surprising, therefore, that parents may show concern about how their child will cope given their past experience and try to do their best to prevent their child from becoming distressed. To your child, however, these signs may show a lack of confidence in his or her ability to cope. Parents might not necessarily act in ways that are as obvious as those in the examples given, but they may try to reduce their child's distress by: (unintentionally) encouraging the child to avoid his or her fears; stepping in to sort out problems for the child; giving a lot of reassurance. All of these are completely natural reactions to a child who is distressed and will all be a help to the child in the short term. The difficulty is that all of these normal, natural behaviors may, in the long term, prevent a child who is very anxious from getting used to new situations, developing skills for dealing with these situations, and overcoming the associated worries and fears.

COPING EXPERIENCES

In order to master fears children need the opportunity to learn that they can tolerate a certain amount of anxiety. This will enable them to enter new situations in which they can learn the skills needed to deal with their anxiety. When a parent is extremely concerned about his or her child becoming anxious and does all he or she can to protect the child from anxiety, the child never gets the opportunity to learn.

Jenny (aged 11)

When Jenny started preschool it was her first experience of anything like that so it was really quite hard for her. When she was a little baby I couldn't see what she would get out of going along to groups. It seemed to be more an opportunity for the mums to get together so I didn't tend to go, as I'm not really that comfortable with that kind of thing. Then as she got older, toddler age and after that, when we did go into any situation where there would be a big group of people she would just get so upset by it that it seemed better to just keep away. She certainly wasn't enjoying being there and she wasn't getting the benefit of it, as she spent the whole time stuck to me.

Jenny's mum's reaction is understandable and demonstrates another way in which the experiences that we have can result from how we are born as well as parental anxieties and expectations. In Jenny's case, as she got older it was simply painful to take her to social activities, as she was such a timid child. Unfortunately, however, this meant that she had little opportunity to get used to being in social groups and to develop the skills to cope with them.

So what has made my child so anxious?

There is clearly no straightforward answer to this question. Various factors influence children's fears and worries, and each of these factors can influence the others. For example, people will respond differently to a child depending on the early personality or experiences that she or he has had. As you can imagine, if a child is known to have been involved in a car accident, carers may be more hesitant about suggesting the child gets into a car and may be more inclined to change their plans if the child is reluctant to get in the car. Equally, the life experiences that a child has will depend in part on how other people respond to him or her. If your child has developed fears and worries, the most important question now, however, is not what has caused these fears and worries but what is keeping them going. This is the focus of the next chapter.

4

What keeps children's fears and worries going?

Sarah (aged 10)

Sarah doesn't actually come across spiders very often, as she makes one of us go into her room if she thinks there might be one so that we can check and get rid of any we find. If she does ever see a spider she just gets away as quickly as she can. She just has this idea that the spider is going to jump up in her face. I think that's pretty unlikely really and I've told her that I'm sure the spider is more scared of her than she is of it, but because she just clears off she never gets to see that the spiders are harmless.

Vicious cycles

Fears and worries are all about vicious cycles. In Chapter 1 we described the three main aspects of anxiety: (i) thinking that something 'bad' might happen; (ii) bodily changes; and (iii) avoidant behavior. Whereas these are the symptoms that make up anxiety itself, they also act to keep each other going. For example, when Sarah comes across a spider, her first thought is 'It's going to jump up in my face and scare me', and her heart starts to beat quickly, giving her more evidence that something bad is going to happen. Not surprisingly she tries to get away. 'Thank goodness,' she thinks, 'it's lucky I got away or that spider would have definitely jumped up in my face.' The next time she comes across a spider the same thing happens again.

The diagrams over the page show some other examples, this time from Tom and Jenny.

Anxious thinking revisited

When people have fears or worries they are likely to have one or both of two common types of thought. The first are thoughts to do with threat: people who are highly anxious tend to *overestimate* how likely it is that something bad is going to happen. Second are thoughts about coping: people who are highly anxious tend to *underestimate* their ability to cope with what might happen.

One part of human nature that can help keep these thoughts going is our tendency to notice things that are going on around us that fit in with our beliefs. For example, imagine a man who has developed a firm belief that people who wear hats when they drive are terrible drivers. Whenever he notices anyone wearing a hat while driving he is on the lookout for any mistake that he or she might make. If he doesn't see him or her make a mistake he discounts this bit of evidence and concludes that he or she must have been concentrating particularly hard at that time, but that he or she is no doubt a terrible driver most of the time. Other drivers may well make mistakes, too, but he is less likely to notice them, as he is not really paying particular attention to what they do. Fears work in exactly the same way. Our attention is firmly focused on noticing and remembering things that confirm the fear, and away from things that do not fit with the fear. If we do see examples that run contrary to our fear-related beliefs we discount them or excuse them in some way. These thinking styles are common, but when they are applied too much of the time and become a habit they can lead to problems.

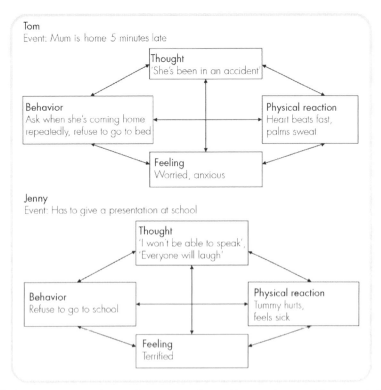

Figure 4.1 Diagrams showing cycle of anxious thoughts, feelings, behavior and physical reactions

Bodily changes revisited

When we consider the anxious thoughts that Tom and Jenny are having in the above examples it is not at all surprising that they are feeling fear and experiencing physical symptoms of fear, such as a racing heart, sweaty palms and an unsettled stomach. These kinds of symptoms can be uncomfortable and alarming, and can lead to even more anxiety. Thus, if a child interprets the physical changes as (i) evidence that something bad is happening; (ii) a sign that something is seriously wrong with his or her body; or (iii) too uncomfortable to bear, then he or she is likely to feel even more fearful and will want to stay away from any situations that could bring on this kind of reaction. In other words, the child starts to fear the bodily symptoms of fear.

Bodily changes can also increase fears and worries by affecting a child's performance. In Jenny's case, for example, shaking, sweating and having a lump in her throat will make it difficult to speak up in front of other people. Being aware of this may make her even less confident about asking a question; then, when the time comes, she will feel even more worried and experience even more physical symptoms. Jenny's fear of not being able to give a presentation was likely to bring about what she most feared: that is, not being able to speak in front of the class.

Anxious behavior revisited

Similarly, when we consider not only the anxious thoughts that Jenny and Tom were having but also the uncomfortable physical sensations that they experienced, it is very understandable why they are behaving the way that they are.

AVOIDANCE
A natural reaction to a threat is to get away from it. In the short term this is the best solution. However, by not facing the feared situation a person never gets to discover whether it really is as bad as he or she fears or learns how to cope with it. By staying home from school, Jenny didn't get to see that it was quite

normal to be nervous about giving presentations. Many of her classmates also showed signs of fear, but this seemed to be understood by the classmates rather than laughed at. She also didn't get a chance to practise and become good at standing up and speaking in front of her peers. As well as more obvious avoidance behaviors children may also avoid in more subtle ways, by doing things in a very particular way that allows them to feel safe. These 'safety behaviors' might include: always having someone with them for support, always carrying a bag in case they are sick, rehearsing what they are going to say in their mind before speaking, or letting their hair cover their face when speaking up. These behaviors help the child feel safe, but in fact they are preventing the child from truly facing his or her fears. This is because after facing a fear he or she is likely to hold a belief such as, 'I asked a question this time but it was only OK because no one could see my face.'

REASSURANCE SEEKING

Like avoidance, getting reassurance from someone else (usually an adult) will make the child feel better right at that moment. If a child is constantly seeking reassurance, however, then it shows that he or she has not used this information to change or update his or her 'fear belief' but has used it for only short-term relief. Imagine a child who, rather than memorizing her spellings, puts them all on to her mobile phone in order to sneakily check them during the spelling test. This will mean that in the future she will not have learned how to spell these words and will still be reliant on her phone or some other way of checking to write them correctly. In the same way, reassurance leads to greater dependence on more reassurance in the future. Yet another vicious cycle!

How other people respond

The way that other people respond to a child can clearly feed into these vicious cycles. In the previous chapter we discussed different ways that children may learn anxious feelings and behaviors from other people around them. If you or other people (other carers, siblings, teachers and so on) are currently responding to your child in any of these ways then this may also be keeping the fears and worries going. In Chapter 3 we specifically talked about (i) learning by example; (ii) learning from other people's reactions to the child; and (iii) having limited opportunities to face fears and develop skills.

To recap, if people around a child are showing signs of fear and responding to these with avoidance, then a child (particularly a sensitive child who may be on the lookout for information that fits with his or her 'fear belief') is likely to learn that the particular object or situation presents a threat and that the best way to respond is by avoiding it. Equally, if carers are responding to a child's attempts at facing fear with particular concern and instead try to encourage the child to keep away from fears, this will also give the child the message that there is something to fear or that he or she will be unable to cope. This would again make the child more likely to adopt an avoidant pattern of behavior. Finally, if a child does not get the opportunities to face fears and test out beliefs then he or she will not get the necessary information to allow him or her to change these fear beliefs and develop the skills needed to become able to deal with challenges independently.

Breaking the cycles

The central aim of the next two chapters of this book is to help you and your child to break the cycles that are keeping his or her fears and worries going. Specifically, should you choose to follow this program, we will be guiding you through ways of working with your child to help him or her adopt a less anxious point of view and to feel confident enough to have a go rather than being put off doing things because of fears. As we have described in this chapter and the last, as a parent or carer you can have a big influence on how your child learns to think and behave. Throughout the next chapters we will, therefore, be helping you to pay attention to how you and other important people in your child's life are responding to his or her anxieties and supporting him or her to develop a new approach to life.

PART TWO

Overcoming Your Child's Fears and Worries

5

A guide to Part Two

Many children experience difficulties with fears and worries at some time or other, and very often families are able to overcome the problems these cause without professional support. For some children the fear seems to just be 'a phase'. For others, the fear may exist but without causing any particular problems for the child or family: they are not having to avoid doing anything they would like to be doing and the child is not bothered by the presence of the fear (for example, a child who is fearful of snakes but rarely comes into contact with them). For others, however, the fears or worries may go on longer or cause more disruption to the child's or family members' lives. The child may frequently be distressed and avoid doing things because of the fear. Members of the family may be working so hard to minimize the child's distress that they are unable to get on with what they would like to be doing. In this situation many families will require specialist help, and it is important that they seek this help and receive it. Many families could, however, if they knew how, overcome these difficulties themselves. This book is designed to help families who are prepared to have a go at helping their child overcome his or her fears and worries themselves but are unsure where to begin.

Before you start

Why change?

It would be understandable if you had some mixed feelings about changing things in your child's, and your own, life. Looking after an anxious child can be distressing in itself, and often exhausting, and it is likely that it has taken a great effort on your part to get by as well as you can and to keep your child's distress to a minimum. We are sure that you will have anticipated that inevitably this program is going to involve your child facing his or her fears. You are likely to have tried this before and may have found that this caused more upset than seemed worthwhile. Maybe, you are thinking, you should just carry on as you are? Maybe he or she will grow out of it? Maybe trying to do something about the situation will just make things worse? These are all understandable reactions to the thought of changing things. Our hunch is that if you are reading this book then things have got to a point where your child's fears or worries are getting in the way to some extent. In many cases children do not grow out of their anxiety problems (although the focus of the anxiety may change). However, there is good research to show that children are likely to overcome anxiety successfully if the principles in this book are used consistently and regularly. Applying these principles may not always be easy; in fact it is very useful to prepare yourself for the reality that there will be obstacles or setbacks along the way. Sometimes things can also seem worse before they seem better, simply because by taking action you are changing the status quo. You need to be aware of this in order to decide whether now is the right time to start overcoming your child's fears and worries.

When to change?

It is worth considering whether now is the right time to be working with your child on his or her anxieties. To be able to apply the principles in this book consistently and regularly will require you to make this your top priority for the next couple of months. If you are about to go on holiday for two weeks, or you are approaching a major deadline at work, you are not going to be able to commit yourself sufficiently to this program. Similarly, if your child is about to go away on a school journey you don't want to make a start that can't be followed up for over a week. In these circumstances, it would be best to postpone starting the program until you are in a position to make this your number-one priority.

Having said that, however, there may always seem to be one reason or another to postpone getting started, but at some time you are going to have to start. So, unless there is a serious reason for not doing so (like those given above), you should set yourself a start date for some time in the near future. What we would suggest is that you get started now by reading through this entire section within the next week or so. You will then have a clear idea of what is going to be involved in order to set your date for getting started with your child.

What to change?

Whereas some children we have worked with seem to experience just one very specific fear, such as dogs, the majority of children experience anxiety about a number of different things. If your child has just one clear fear then there will be no problem for you in deciding what to focus your work on. If, however, your child seems to worry about all kinds of things you will need to decide early on what you are going to make your focus. It is very important that you do choose *one* particular fear or worry to focus upon. This keeps things simpler for you and your child, and the gains that are made will be clear and obvious to you both. You may feel that by picking one fear you are dealing with just 'the tip of the iceberg', but this need not put you off, for two reasons. First, skills will be learned and practised by you and your child. It will then be easier to apply them to other fears (one by one). Second, having success at overcoming one fear will teach your child some valuable lessons, which will have knock-on effects for other fears: (i) that fears can be overcome; and (ii) that she or he is capable of overcoming them.

About the self-help program

The following chapters introduce you to the most important part of the program: the steps you can use to overcome your child's fears and worries. These are the basic elements of cognitive behavior therapy (CBT) for children with anxiety problems. CBT refers to treatment based on the premise that how we think about things is associated with how we behave and how we feel. Therefore, by changing how we think about our fears and how we act because of them we can change how we feel about them. This type of therapy is widely used with adults and children and has, in the last decade, become a treatment of choice for many emotional problems, particularly anxiety difficulties. A number of treatment studies have shown that where the principles described in this book are followed consistently, children benefit considerably.

The five steps

The five main principles are shown in the box on the facing page. These principles can also be treated as steps, as they follow each other in the order that is given.

Step 1 Learning to spot your child's anxious thoughts
(Asking the right questions and listening to the answers)

↓

Step 2 Helping your child to evaluate the thought and consider other points of view
(Asking the right questions to help your child work out if the thought is reasonable and/or helpful. Helping your child to test out other ways of thinking about the fear)

↓

Step 3 Encouraging independence and 'having a go'
(Using praise and rewards to encourage non-anxious behavior)

↓

Step 4 Developing a step-by-step plan with your child
(Helping your child to make a plan for gradually facing his or her fears)

↓

Step 5 Problem solving
(Asking the right questions to help your child become an independent problem-solver)

In addition to the five steps shown in the box, two sets of principles are described in chapters at the end of this Part. Chapter 11 provides guidelines on what you can do if your child is a worrier – for example, if worry itself seems to have taken on a life of its own and has become hard for your child to control. If this does apply to your child then we would recommend applying these principles throughout the whole course of your program (that is, while you are working through the five steps).

Chapter 12 concerns managing your own anxiety. It is clearly not always the case, but the majority of parents who we work with also experience difficulties with anxiety themselves. It has been found that where parents are very anxious themselves, if their anxiety is dealt with first the child is more likely to benefit from treatment. This could be because if you are less anxious your child will start to learn other ways of thinking and behaving from you and you will also find it less difficult to follow this program. If you are an anxious person yourself, by making a concerted effort to overcome this you will not only be helping yourself but also helping your child to become less anxious. Again, we would encourage you to read Chapter 12 before you embark upon the five steps.

Addressing particular needs

In Part Three additional techniques are described that may or may not apply to you and your child, depending on the nature of your child's fears. These concern night-time problems, school problems, relaxation, and managing difficult behavior.

The main sections of this book use case examples and material that are most directly relevant to mid-childhood (ages six to 12 years). Two chapters are, however, devoted to discussing what you will need to take into account if your child is outside this age group. We would recommend that you read Chapter 14 if your child is eight years of age or younger and Chapter 15 if your child is about 11 years or older. If either of these chapters applies to your child, we suggest you read it before you embark upon the five steps and to apply the principles throughout the whole course of your program.

How to use this guide

Throughout this program the emphasis is on you helping your child to overcome his or her anxieties. Rather than solving problems for your child, or reassuring him or her that everything will be fine, your role will be to act as both coach and cheerleader. You will be in charge of helping your child to work out what to do for him- or herself and then cheering on his or her progress. At the end of the day it will be your child who has to deal with problems; you cannot guarantee that you'll always be there when a problem arises, so it is essential that your child is learning, with help from you, how to deal with fears and worries on his or her own. Nonetheless, it is quite likely that you see your child's fears and worries as a bigger problem than your child does. For example, if a child feels nervous about attending school he or she is unlikely to think that the answer is to overcome this fear and go to school. Instead, he or she will think that the best thing to do is simply not go to school. Although you need to work with and guide your child, it is also your responsibility to take the lead, encourage, motivate and set a good example to your child. Throughout this section we will consider ways of encouraging your child to get involved. There are also additional tips in Chapter 15 for increasing motivation while using this book with adolescents.

As you can see from the table of steps, much of your job involves asking your child questions to help him or her work things out for him- or herself. To do this successfully you need to be asking the right questions. This is not always easy, but we will help you. It is essential that the questions are asked in a way that shows your child you are taking his or her worries seriously – that you are not making fun or being critical. This can be difficult at times, particularly if you are feeling frustrated by your child's behavior. For your child to work with you, you need to show that you understand and accept what your child is worried about. However, you also need to communicate that you recognize that this worry is getting in the way and so something needs to be done about it.

Whereas the worries themselves need to be taken seriously, in working together to overcome them you can enjoy yourselves. Take every opportunity to have fun and be creative. If the whole program is heavy and emotional your child is not going to want to be involved; so when it comes to Chapter 8 (Step 3) onwards, try to lighten the mood and enjoy yourselves!

Keeping written records

Throughout the book we ask you to keep records of the work that you do with your child. Some parents like to work through these with their children whereas others sit down later and complete them. Either way it is essential that you do put pen to paper and complete them, for two reasons. First, writing things down helps learning and remembering. Second, this allows you to look back later to see where you had got to. Often parents will feel as if things have been moving backwards, but then when they actually look at their written records they see that progress has been made. It is easy to feel that what is happening right now has been happening forever, but this is generally not the case. (As with all the charts we use in the book, not all of the questions will be relevant to your particular situation; just answer those that apply to your own or your child's experiences, as applicable.)

You don't need to go it alone

We often work with single parents who put this program into practice very successfully on their own. There is no doubt, however, that it will be easier to work through the program with your child if you have help from others around you. This may be a partner, parent, older child, a friend or your child's teacher. The more people around your child following the same principles, the easier it will be for your child to learn how to overcome fears and worries. Equally, working with another adult is likely to motivate you and keep you going at times when it feels like a struggle. Also, as we mentioned above, this program includes practising ways of talking to your child to help him or her – for example, explaining what his or her worry is and to consider other ways of thinking. Sometimes the strategies that we suggest may be tricky. In particular it can be difficult to stick to asking questions rather than giving your child reassurance or trying to solve problems for him or her. You may feel embarrassed at first, but having a practise run at these conversations with another adult will help prepare you for talking through these things with your child. Your 'partner' can help you work out which questions worked well, whether the tone was right and whether your child would feel understood and taken seriously.

Keeping it going

The final chapter in this section is all about keeping your child's progress going. It is likely that having read all the way through this book you will feel charged up and ready to go and tackle your child's difficulties. It is just as likely that this feeling will plummet when you hit your first hurdle. You may feel that you have failed, that you're not doing it properly and that your child will never recover. It is really important to stress that if overcoming your child's problems were easy, you would have done it long ago. You must be prepared for the fact that there *will* be setbacks – times when your child does not make as much progress as you had hoped, or even seems to go backwards. Be reassured that this is normal. Your child has been in a pattern of thinking, behaving and feeling a certain way for some time – this is not going to change overnight. However, if you follow the principles described here you will be helping your child to take control of these fears or worries and you will almost certainly make progress.

So now it is time to take your first step and read what is involved in helping your child overcome his or her fears and worries.

Good luck!

6

Step 1: Spotting anxious thinking

Note: Read through all of Step 1 before trying to put any of the strategies into place.

As we discussed earlier, children who are very anxious tend to think about things in a particular way. You may have noticed that your child tends to see danger all around him or her. For example, imagine you had been out to the shops without your child and were caught in traffic on the way home. For some children this situation would cause enormous anxiety. This is not surprising considering that, to the child who worries about separating from his or her parents, the fact that the parent was late home was a likely sign that he or she had been injured or even killed.

Seeing danger everywhere

Anxious children are 'on the lookout' for threat and 'jump to conclusions' about threat, and if what is going on is not absolutely clear they will interpret the situation as threatening. Also, a more anxious child will think that he or she is not going to be able to deal with the dangers thrown at him or her, and is likely to become extremely distressed. These ways of thinking are associated with anxiety even in young children (from preschool age), so we would recommend having a go at the tasks in this chapter with any child who can talk about his or her fears. If your child is young (say eight years of age or younger), or struggles with what you are trying to work on with him or her, then you should find Chapter 14 helpful, as this focuses specifically on making the strategies in this book more suitable for younger children.

Helpful and unhelpful thoughts

Here is an example. Jenny has to give a presentation at school tomorrow. She thinks that she won't be able to do it. She expects that she will get extremely scared and won't be able to think of what to say. All the other children will laugh at her and think she is stupid. No wonder she feels anxious! And no wonder that she will probably feel quite sick before school and won't want to go in. Philippa also has to give a presentation at school tomorrow. She feels a bit nervous about it, too, but she thinks that everyone will probably get a bit nervous doing the presentation so the rest of the class will understand how she feels. She thinks it will probably be fine, but if not it will soon be over and forgotten about. The next day Philippa feels a little nervous but goes in to school and has a go at the presentation.

From these examples illustrated in the figure opposite, we can see that different thoughts are associated with different feelings and different actions. Some thoughts can be quite helpful: they help us feel calm and stop us missing out on things. Other thoughts can be unhelpful: they make us more anxious and stop us having a go at things that we might enjoy or that might be good for us.

How do I know what my child is thinking?

If you are not sure what your child is thinking in this situation, try asking him or her. This may seem like an easy task, and for some parents and children it is, but for others it can be quite tricky. One reason is that your child may not really know why he or she is worried; sometimes these thoughts pop into our heads so quickly that we hardly notice them. For that reason it is useful to try to ask your child about his or her worries as they happen, rather than much later on.

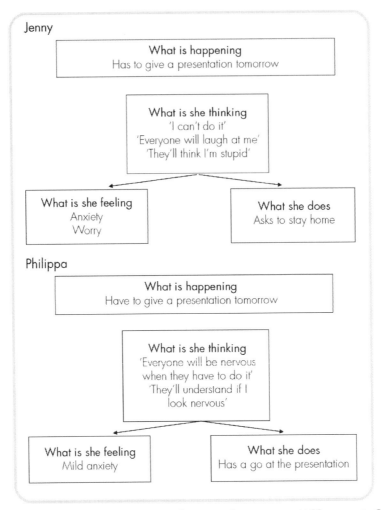

Figure 6.1 How different thoughts relate to different feelings and actions

On the other hand, your child may know what he or she is worried about but may find it hard to tell you as, perhaps, other people are present and this makes him or her feel self-conscious. This may mean you cannot ask about the worries immediately, at the time of anxiety. In this case try to create a comfortable environment to talk to your child as soon as possible after the event.

Asking questions

The box below gives some examples of questions you can ask to help your child tell you what it is that worries him or her. Use these questions when you spot signs that your child is feeling anxious (such as from his or her behavior or from bodily symptoms).

BOX 6.1 SPOTTING UNHELPFUL THOUGHTS

Example questions to ask:

'Why are you worried?'

'What is frightening you?'

'What do you think will happen?'

'What is it about [this situation] that is making you worried?'

Clearly, there is nothing very clever or magical about these questions. But there are two main points to keep in mind. First, these questions all start with 'What' or 'Why'. These are called 'open' questions. Compare these to what are called 'closed' questions – for example: 'Do you worry that you will get hurt?', 'Are you worried that the dog will bite you?'. To closed questions your child can just give you a yes or no answer, which may not help you very much as you try to get a better understanding of how he or she is thinking. Open questions, on the other hand, do not limit the response in this way, and you are likely to get a lot more helpful information. We would recommend you try to stick to open questions as much as possible.

Second, think about *how* you ask these questions. Think about different ways of asking the first question. How you ask the question should give your child the message that you can see that he or she is worried and that you want to help. In contrast, asking 'Why [on earth!] are you worried?' may make a child much more reluctant to answer, as there is a clear message that he or she really should not be worried in this situation and that he or she is bad or silly for thinking the way he or she does.

If that doesn't work

In order to tell you about his or her thoughts a child must firmly believe that you are asking because you want to understand the worries better in order to help him or her. It may be that the first time you ask these questions your child is reluctant to express his or her fears. But as you continue to ask these kinds of questions in situations in which your child is fearful he or she might find it easier to begin to answer.

If you feel you have been asking these questions for a while and in each situation you have exhausted your open questions, then you may need to encourage your child by talking about what types of things might make *you* worry in a similar situation. For example,

Ben didn't want to be upstairs when everyone else in the house was downstairs. The following discussion went on between Ben and his father.

Dad: 'Ben, could you just pop upstairs and get your shoes?'

Ben: 'No.'

Dad: 'What is it that worries you about going upstairs?'

Ben: 'I don't want to go on my own.'

Dad: 'But why is that? What do you think will happen when you are up there?'

Ben: 'Nobody will be up there with me.'

Dad: 'But why does that worry you?'

Ben: 'I don't know.'

Dad: 'I suppose if I had to go up on my own, I might be worried that if I fell over no one would be there to help me up. Is that what you are worried about?'

When his father asked him what worried him about being upstairs alone, Ben's response was to give details of the situation that worried him, but what his dad really needed to know was what Ben thought was going to happen. To this, as we have seen, he initially replied, 'I don't know'. However, his dad then tentatively suggested possibilities to get the ball rolling and help Ben describe his fear. In Ben's case his worry was quite different from what his dad had suggested (it was actually to do with a character he had seen in a film coming to get him when nobody else was there), but his dad making suggestions in a non-judgmental manner helped Ben to feel that his dad would not be cross with him when he found out what he feared.

Making suggestions based on what you might fear also shows children that it is not necessarily 'abnormal' to worry about a situation. Other people are likely to worry about it, too. Children often feel as if they are the only ones who worry about a particular thing, but realizing that this is not true can make it much easier for them to start to talk about the worries.

'But hang on,' you may now be thinking, 'if I make suggestions to my child, won't that just give my child a whole load of new things to worry about?' Our experience is that this does not happen. Children tend to have quite specific worries and fears and they generally don't 'catch' worries from others.

Sometimes children may report that they are not frightened of anything in particular, but that they are worried that they will get a frightened feeling. In this case, find out more about your child's thoughts about having this feeling. What if he or she does get that feeling? What would happen then? What is the worst that could happen? There are still likely to be frightening thoughts associated with the presence of this feeling – for example, 'I'll get a scared feeling and lose control and make a fool of myself', 'I will be sick and everyone will look at me and think I'm disgusting.'

Checking that you've understood

If you already have an idea in your mind about what scares your child then it can be easy to draw quick conclusions about what your child is telling you. To make sure you have absolutely understood what is worrying your child you need to tell him or her what you understand from what he or she has told you, and give him or her the opportunity to correct you if you've got it wrong.

An example from Ben and his dad is overleaf.

A final point to make about Step 1 is that you will see, in the example given, that although Ben's dad is showing that he can understand why Ben is so worried, he does not ever say that it is right or wrong for Ben to be worried. What he does say is that he can understand why Ben is worried *given the frightening thoughts that he is having.* The implication here is that if Ben is going to be less worried, something needs to be done about those thoughts. This takes us nicely on to the next step.

Dad: 'OK, thank you. I think I understand better now, but can I just check with you?'

Ben: 'Yeah, OK.'

Dad: 'So the thing that is most frightening about going upstairs on your own is that no one will be there with you; and that is scary because in the film that you saw that monster, Drog, was coming after children when their parents weren't around. Is that right?'

Ben: 'Yeah, pretty much.'

Dad: 'Oh, is it not quite right?'

Ben: 'Well, it's not just their parents. It's when anyone's not around. So it's OK if Julie's with me. Drog wouldn't come then.'

Dad: 'Oh I see. So the main thing is that if you are on your own upstairs then you think Drog may come and take you?'

Ben: 'Yes, he'd take me to his cave and then I wouldn't see any of you again.'

Dad: 'I see. That does sound very frightening if you are thinking that if you go up on your own Drog will come and take you and then you'll never see us again. I think I can really understand it now. Do you think I've got it right?'

Ben: 'Yes, that's right.'

Your child's thoughts

Have a go at completing the diagram Figure 6.2 for a situation that your child finds frightening.

From this exercise we hope that the way your child behaves in certain situations starts to make more sense. At times it may seem that he or she is behaving irrationally, but when we take into account what he or she is thinking in that situation, his or her behavior is likely to make perfect sense.

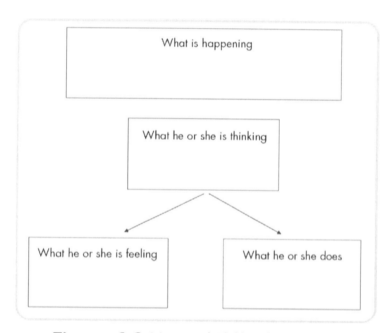

Figure 6.2 Your child's thoughts

STEP 1: KEY POINTS

• Ask your child to express what is worrying him or her during the event or as soon as possible afterwards.

- Make the *way* you ask the question show your interest and support.

- Keep an open mind about your child's thoughts. Don't assume you know what he or she is worried about.

- Keep questions open – use 'What' and 'Why'.

- If necessary make suggestions: what might worry you about this situation?

- When you think you have understood what your child is afraid of, check this out by repeating it back to him or her to make sure you have understood it correctly.

7

Step 2: Is that a helpful thought?

Note: Read through all of Step 2 before trying to put any of the strategies into place.

At this point you will have a clear idea of what your child is thinking in the situations that make him or her scared or nervous. The next step is to set about helping your child to work out whether the thought is a helpful one, or whether there may be other ways of thinking about the situation that may be more helpful to him or her in overcoming his or her fears and worries. In this chapter we will talk you through the basic steps. However, if you can be creative and find a way to make this apply particularly to your child and his or her interests then your child will relate to it and enjoy it more, both of which are going to increase your chances of success.

There are three steps for helping your child to evaluate his or her anxious thoughts. These are described in the boxes on the following pages.

Thinking like a judge in court

You can see that following these steps is rather like being a judge in a court of law: first identifying a suspect (the offending thought), then considering the evidence and checking up on other possible suspects (other ways of thinking about this situation), before making a judgment about whether you were right about that first suspect (is the thought helpful/realistic?). How a judge works in solving crimes is often familiar to children from television programs or films, so you may be able to take advantage of this to help make this process appealing to your child. If not a judge, is there some other crime-fighting or problem-solving character that appeals to your child? If you are not sure, just ask your child who he or she would call in if he or she needed to solve a problem, or make tentative suggestions, as Jenny's mum did in the example on the following pages (with an initially reluctant Jenny). This is where your creativity comes in!

BOX 7.1 STEPS FOR EVALUATING THE THOUGHT

1 What is the evidence to support that thought?

Help your child to look for the evidence for the thought and work out whether this evidence is (i) realistic or unrealistic; and (ii) helpful or unhelpful.

Example questions to ask:

'What makes you think that [the feared situation] will happen?'

'Has that ever happened to you before?'

'Have you ever seen that happen to someone else?'

'How likely is it that [the feared situation] will happen?'

Tips to remember:

1 Choose the thought that causes your child the most anxiety.

2 Work as a team: show your interest in what your child has to say.

3 If your child doesn't know what will happen, encourage him or her to find out by setting up an experiment.

2 Considering alternative thoughts

Next, you need to help your child to work out whether there are any other ways to think about this situation.

Example questions to ask:

'Can you imagine that anything else could happen?'

'If [the feared situation] did happen, could there be any other reasons for it?'

'What would you think was happening if someone else was in the same boat?'

'What would [another child] think if [he or she] was in this situation?'

Tips to remember:

4 Give your child the chance to come up with helpful thoughts him- or herself.

5 If necessary, offer your child some suggestions to get the ball rolling.

6 Take all your child's ideas seriously and praise his or her efforts.

3 Help your child come to conclusions

So, all in all, what does your child think now that he or she has considered different ways of thinking about this situation? Even if he or she still thinks that something bad will happen, how likely does he or she think it will be? Your child may not draw the same conclusions that you might, but this doesn't matter. The main thing is that your child has had practise at thinking about situations in ways other than the 'automatic' anxious way.

Tips to remember:

7 It can be tempting to draw conclusions for your child, but try to hold back.

8 Your child thinking this through by him- or herself will help him or her remember the conclusions and the procedure.

Asking questions, not giving answers

You will notice that in the example Jenny's mum asked Jenny lots of questions to help her work out other ways of thinking about the situation that she feared. This contrasts with the example following.

Jenny

Mum: 'Jenny, you seem really upset about going into school tomorrow. What's up?'

Jenny: 'Nothing. I just don't feel right.'

Mum: 'So it looks like we've got a problem here. If we had a problem to solve and we could call on anyone at all to help us, who do you think it should be? Who could help us solve a really tricky problem?'

Jenny: 'I don't know.'

Mum: 'What about Harry Potter?'

Jenny: 'No Mum, I don't think so.'

Mum: 'OK. So who could it be? What about Miss Marple? You like watching her when they put the films on in the afternoon.'

Jenny: 'If you say so.'

Mum: 'So let's imagine Miss Marple is here. I guess first she's going to have to know what the problem is. So we're going to have to tell her what it is about going to school tomorrow that is scary. What shall we tell her?'

Jenny: 'Ummmm...'

Mum: 'Maybe there's been a murder in the library?'

Jenny: 'Yes.'

Mum: 'Is that what is worrying about going tomorrow?'

Tom: 'No. Don't be silly. It's just that there is a supply teacher coming tomorrow.'

Mum: 'OK, and what do you think will happen?'

Jenny: 'They won't know that I need help with my maths and will get cross with me.'

Mum: 'I see. That does sound worrying. So we need Miss Marple to help us work out if that really is going to happen. So how could she do that?'

Jenny: 'She could go into the future and look.'

Mum: 'Maybe she could, or maybe she could look at the past?

What has happened before when there has been a supply teacher?'

Jenny: 'One time the supply teacher asked me a really difficult question and I didn't know the answer and he shouted at me and everyone thought I was stupid.'

Mum: 'Oh, that sounds horrible. Has that happened every time you've had a supply teacher?'

Jenny: 'No, only that time.'

Mum: 'And do you have supply teachers very often?'

Jenny: 'Yeah, quite a lot.'

Mum: 'And have other supply teachers ever asked you questions?'

Jenny: 'Not much, but sometimes.'

Mum: 'And what has happened?'

Jenny: 'Sometimes I know the answer, if it's easy. Sometimes I don't, but nothing happened.'

Mum: 'OK. We have told Miss Marple that one time a teacher did get cross when you couldn't answer a question, but that was just one teacher out of a lot of supply teachers that you have had. And mostly when they have asked you a question it's been OK. Is that right?'

Jenny: 'Yeah.'

Mum: 'And if a supply teacher did get cross, everyone might think you were stupid. Or might they think anything else? Miss Marple needs to know if there are any other possibilities before she can decide what you should do. What would you think if the teacher shouted at one of your friends because they got a question wrong?'

Jenny: 'I'd think that the question was really hard, or maybe my friend was just thinking about something else for a minute.'

Mum: 'That's a really good point. So what do you think Miss Marple would say about going to school tomorrow when there will be a supply teacher there?'

Jenny: 'She might say that most of the supply teachers are really nice and even if they do shout it doesn't mean you're stupid.'

Tom

Dad: 'Tom, what is it that worries you so much about sleeping in your own bed?'

Tom: 'I don't want to be on my own.'

Dad: 'Oh come on, Tom. You'll be fine on your own. Nothing has ever happened to you when you've been in your room and your mum and me are right in the room next door.'

There are a number of reasons why asking your child questions to help him or her work out a new way of thinking for him- or herself is likely to work out better than trying to talk your child out of the fear as Tom's dad does. The first is that if your child is able to think this through for himor herself then he or she will be in a better position when something scary happens and you are not there. If he or she relies on you for reassurance, he or she is likely to panic when there is a need to act and think independently. Also, children remember what they have learned better if they were helped to work it out for themselves rather than just being told. By having your help to think through his or her fears, this method of considering the evidence and alternative ways of thinking will become second nature to your child. Finally, as you can see from the example, asking children questions to help them think things through encourages them to get involved in fighting their own fears, and it puts them in a position of control (as opposed to feeling out of control, which is common among people when they feel anxious). In contrast, just telling your child why he or she shouldn't think the way he or she does makes him or her feel that he or she is doing something wrong, is stupid and is being told off!

Practise first

Using questions in a gentle and interested way to help a child think through worries can be a tricky thing to do. We can easily be tempted to supply the answers or end up sounding judgmental about the answers that we are given. For this reason, before you have a go at this with your child, try to find a willing volunteer who you can practise with – for example, a partner, friend or relative. Ask the person to imagine that he or she is your child and tell him or her which fear you would like him or her to pretend to have. Then try working through Table 7.1: Helping my child with unhelpful thoughts (at the end of this chapter), with him or her. If you get stuck, try swapping over and letting your helper be you, and you can be your child. See if this gives you pause for thought or any new ideas. Once you have practised, give this a try with your child. Don't worry if it doesn't go perfectly first time – it does no harm to show your child an example that practise makes perfect!

Test out the fears

Sometimes children may not really know that what they fear will happen, they just don't like the idea of doing something, or they may just have a bad feeling about it. Or they may not know whether the fear they hold is realistic or not, as they don't have any information to go on. At other times your child may be able to think through the fear but end up feeling that he or she shouldn't feel nervous, but still does. In all of these situations help your child put the fears to the test. Your child will no doubt be familiar with experiments from doing science at school. Your job now is to work with him or her to design an experiment to find out if what he or she fears is true. Some examples are given in the box opposite.

BOX 7.2 EXPERIMENTS TO TEST FEARS

1 If I give the wrong answer in class everyone will think I'm stupid.

Experiment: keep a record of every time anyone gives a wrong answer in class during one day. Rate (from 0 to 5) how stupid I think each person is whenever it happens.

2 If I see a dog in the street it will bite me.

Experiment: find out from searching the Internet how many people in the UK have dogs as pets and how many get bitten each year.

3 If my homework has any mistakes in it I will get into big trouble.

Experiment: make a deliberate mistake in my homework and record what happens.

4 If I go near a spider it will jump in my face.

Experiment: look up spiders in the library and find out how high they can jump.

If you set up experiments and put fears to the test your child is more likely to remember the conclusions. Using practical exercises like this also helps the child to *feel* differently, not just to think differently.

An essential thing to remember is that if you set up an experiment with your child you *must* remember to ask him or her how it has gone and help him or her to work out what the results mean. Use the results to add information to the thought record that you are working on with your child. Your child needs to feel that all the trouble was worth the effort and that it was a useful thing to do, if you ever want him or her to try anything like that again!

Cutting out reassurance

Going through this process clearly takes more time than just saying 'There's nothing to worry about', 'You'll be fine' or even 'Just get on with it'. Such responses may well be our instinctive reactions, but that approach does not work. In fact, particularly for highly anxious children, reassurance actually stops them being able to manage situations on their own. For example, a child who is always told, 'It's OK. Mummy's here'; can hardly be blamed for panicking when he or she runs into problems when Mummy's not there! Reassurance is often going to be a parent's natural reaction to their child's anxiety. But if your child is having problems with anxiety you must try to cut out the reassurance and instead work with him or her to help find ways to reassure him- or herself.

Actual and ongoing threat

A final, but important, point to mention here is that as you become clearer on the details of what your child worries about it may become apparent that there *is* a clear and actual threat to your child. An example is a child who is scared to go to school because he or she is being bullied. In order for the child to feel differently about going to school it is crucial that this problem is solved first of all. On discovering such a clear, objective threat, it is crucial that you take positive action to eliminate the threat. It makes no sense for a child to 'think positively' about bullying. However, even in a situation like this we would encourage you to involve the child in the problem-solving process, although the extent to which we can do this depends, of course, on the nature of the situation. Chapter 10 gives more information on involving your child in overcoming problems. Chapter 18 talks specifically about bullying. If your child tends to think there is danger all around him or her and that nothing can be done about it, it is important to show him or her that if he or she does come across a real danger something can be done.

The written record

At the end of this chapter you will find a record form to note down how you get on with the tasks described in this chapter, specifically to note down (i) what was happening that triggered your child's fear or worry,

(ii) how your child responded to your questions or experiments, and (iii) the outcome: how your child thought, felt and behaved in the end. (As with all the charts we use in the book, not all of the questions will be relevant to your particular situation; just answer those that apply to your or your child's experiences.)

STEP 2: KEY POINTS

• Once you know what your child is frightened of:

• Show that you are interested in your child's point of view and take it seriously.

• Discover, with your child, what makes him or her hold this thought.

• Help your child consider other points of view.

• Help your child conduct experiments to put his or her fear to the test.

• Hold back reassurance.

• Be creative and make it fun where possible!

TABLE 7.1: HELPING MY CHILD WITH UNHELPFUL THOUGHTS

What is happening?	What is he or she thinking?	Evidence and alternatives	What happened in the end?
	Why are you worried? What do you think will happen? What is it about this situation that is making you worried?	What makes you think that [this situation] will happen? Has that ever happened to you before? Have you ever been that happen to someone else? How likely is it that [this situation] will happen? Can you imagine that anything else could happen? If [this situation] did happen, could there be any other reasons for it? What would you think was happening if someone else was in the same boat? What would [another child] think if they were in this situation? How could you test out this thought?	What did your child think? What did your child do? How did your child feel?

An additional copy can be found in Appendix 2.

8

Step 3: Encouraging independence and 'having a go'

Note: Read through all of Step 3 before trying to put any of the strategies into place.

The first two steps have focused upon anxious or unhelpful thoughts, in particular how thoughts can influence feelings and behavior. By now you will have discussed with your child what it is that worries him or her about particular situations, and you will have started to take some steps towards new ways of thinking about these situations. You may have found that your child has been able to think differently about the fears and, as a result, he or she may have already started to behave differently. For some children this can be the key step. For others, however, they may be starting to think about the situation differently but they still don't actually want to confront that situation. Maybe this isn't surprising if avoiding the fear is a habit they have had for a long time. In this chapter and the next we are going to talk about ways to encourage your child to 'have a go', rather than to avoid their fears and worries.

Encouraging 'having a go'

As we have already said, if a person feels anxious he or she is more likely to try to avoid the source of the anxiety, rather than confront it. In many ways this seems to be a sensible strategy. For example, if Jenny believes that by asking her teacher a question she will show her classmates how stupid she is, make a fool of herself or be ridiculed, then it's not at all surprising that she won't want to put her hand up in class. The difficulty is, however, that because Jenny never puts her hand up in class she never finds out whether her belief is true or whether, in fact, her classmates wouldn't even bat an eyelid. Reducing avoidance and learning to 'have a go' is, therefore, crucial for overcoming anxiety. Given your child's fears and worries he or she is going to need some encouragement in order to 'have a go'. The following strategies will help you to do this.

Attention and praise

Giving attention and praise is probably the most effective way to influence children's behavior. Praise needs to be clear and specific so that your child understands exactly what it is that he or she has done that you are so pleased about. The extracts from conversations between Jenny and her mum on the following page show examples of clear and specific praise.

Being on the lookout for 'have a go' behavior

Parenting an anxious child can be extremely difficult and, because of your worries about your child, you are likely to have become very focused on the things that are making him or her upset or the things that he or she can't or won't do. This is an entirely natural reaction but it can lead to a vicious cycle in which a child's anxious behavior is receiving a lot of attention while non-anxious, 'have a go' behavior is, inadvertently, being ignored. This is what happened between Ben and his parents, as shown in the diagram on the following page.

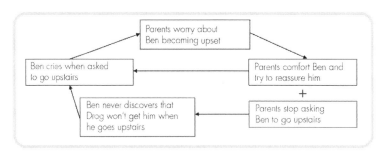

Figure 8.1 Cycle created when the focus is on avoidance rather than 'have a go' behavior

BOX 8.1 ENCOURAGING JENNY TO HAVE A GO

General and vague: 'Well done, Jenny.'

Clear and specific: 'Jenny, you did so well this morning when you got up and got ready for school without becoming upset. I know Monday can be a worrying day for you so I was really proud of how you just got up and got on with it!'

General and vague: 'Your teacher told me you did well today. That's great!'

Clear and specific: 'Your teacher told me that you asked a question in class today, Jenny. I bet that was quite a scary thing to do, but you didn't let that stop you. Well done!'

You need to shift that balance, and weigh attention more heavily on your child's attempts at facing fears, and praise these at every opportunity.

Although this all sounds simple enough, it can be quite difficult at times, as it involves looking out for and noticing your child behaving in a way that might be taken for granted with another child. For example, as you will remember, Ben was worried about going upstairs on his own. Every now and again Ben did manage to make a quick trip upstairs to grab something before running back down. This behavior had been so swift but also so 'normal' (by other people's standards) that it had generally passed without comment. Once Ben's parents became more aware of this behavior, they had two other concerns about praising it. First, they worried that they might make Ben more aware that sometimes he was facing his fear, which may make it more of a big deal and actually make him more reluctant to do it. Second,

Ben's brothers were running up and down the stairs all the time and they weren't getting praise for it. It seemed unfair to be giving praise just to Ben. Ben's parents, however, 'had a go' at praising Ben's efforts. They found that rather than the praise making Ben more aware that he was sometimes going up the stairs (and more nervous about it), Ben really appreciated it and that it seemed to boost his confidence that he could go up the stairs without anything terrible happening. Ben's brothers appreciated that he had difficulties going upstairs so didn't seem to think there was anything unfair about Ben being praised for his attempt. In fact they started to join in giving him praise themselves. Soon particular things started to stand out which each brother struggled to do (for one it was getting up in good time for school, and for the other it was getting homework done on time), so each boy started to receive praise for his own particular challenge.

Rewards

In addition to praise, when children achieve specific goals, giving rewards is an effective way of letting them know how much you appreciate what they have done and encouraging them to continue with that sort of behavior. Rewards don't need to be expensive; in fact they don't need to cost money at all. We are often struck by what rewards children come up with when asked to think of them. For example, Ben chose

'Going to the park with Daddy' and Jenny chose 'Making cakes with Mum' among their rewards.

HAVING A RANGE OF REWARDS TO SUIT DIFFERENT ACHIEVEMENTS

You and your child will need to come up with a range of rewards to suit different goals. For example, if you were to reward a small goal with a huge reward then what will you do when your child achieves a huge goal? The box on the facing page provides a space for you and your child to come up with a list of rewards together. Put down only those things upon which you both agree. For example, there is no point in offering your child a trip to the cinema if he or she hates the cinema; equally there is no point in setting up the trip of a lifetime as a reward if it may be unlikely to happen!

IMMEDIATE REWARDS

Try to come up with rewards that you are able to give to your child immediately or very soon after he or she has made the achievement so that it is very clear what has earned him or her the reward. A reward also needs to be something that you will be happy *not* to give your child if the goal is not achieved. What would be the point of your child going to the trouble of facing the fear if he or she could have got that reward anyway? An example of a reward that is likely not to work out is 'If you can get to school on time every day this term we'll all go on a family holiday in the summer'. The first reason that this is unlikely to reinforce your child's 'have a go' behavior is that the promised reward is too distant in the future. It will mean he or she may have, for example, faced the fear for a whole week with nothing good seeming to have happened at all. Children are rarely able to see such a distant event as an incentive. Second, it is likely that the holiday will need to be booked before the goal has been achieved and that it will be very hard to not go should the goal not be met! This reward is also a very big deal! If your child had an even bigger goal to aim for in the future, how would you top that? Finally, the whole family's holiday resting on his or her performance puts a lot of pressure on the child and, understandably, siblings would be very annoyed if the family holiday was cancelled. The consequences of this are likely to be negative for your child. Rewards, as we have discussed, act as a bonus.

BOX 8.2 PRAISE AND REWARDS

Tips to remember:

- Make praise clear and specific.

- Include a range of rewards under each category.

- Rewards don't need to be expensive.

- Make sure both you and your child agree to the reward.

- Make sure you would be happy not to give the reward if the goal was not met.

> • Try to have rewards that can be given immediately or soon after the goal has been met.
>
> **Things to say to my child:**
>
> **Things to do with my child:**
>
> **Other things my child would enjoy:**

PROBLEMS WITH GIVING REWARDS

Parents sometimes have concerns about giving rewards to their children. The box below lists some of the common concerns that parents raise, along with our responses to them.

BOX 8.3 PARENTS' CONCERNS ABOUT REWARDS

1 I don't want to bribe my child to do what I want him or her to do.

Sometimes parents feel as if they are manipulating their child by giving rewards and they think that this is wrong. We would agree that this is wrong if the child is being 'rewarded' for doing something that benefits the parent and not the child. Here, however, we are using rewards to help the child to do something specifically because it will benefit him or her in the future. As far as Jenny was concerned, asking the teacher a question could have only bad consequences (such as looking silly in front of her peers). Her parents, however, as adults, were in a position to see that in the long term she would benefit both academically and socially by being able to speak up in front of her peers. The reward they gave said; 'I appreciate that was hard for you, so well done for doing it.' The promise of the reward also tipped the balance for Jenny as, in addition to the various negative consequences that she could imagine, there was now something clearly positive to be gained that would happen soon.

2 If I start rewarding this behavior I'll have to keep rewarding it forever.

It is true that when you have identified a behavior as deserving a reward you do want to be on the lookout for that behavior so you can be consistent in rewarding it. As we have said above, however, rewards are used to help children do something that would otherwise be difficult to face. Once that task becomes easy (or even boring) it no longer requires a reward, and it is time to shift the rewards to other goals (see Chapter 9: on taking a step-by-step approach). The end of giving a reward for a particular behavior can be framed as a positive thing, as Jenny's mum said to her: 'You're so good at asking your teacher for help after the lesson now that I don't need to give you a reward for that, but asking for help *during* the class will definitely deserve a reward!'

3 It's unfair on my other children who do this behavior without needing rewards.

As we mentioned with regard to praise, children are able to understand that different children deserve rewards for different things, as they all have different things that they find a challenge. One family that we recently worked with had a great system in which the whole family earned rewards, and whenever any one of them achieved his or her particular goal pebbles would be placed in a jar. When the jar was full the whole family would have a shared reward, such as a family outing.

4 Why should I reward 'normal behavior'?

Although the behavior you are hoping to see may be 'normal' for many children, for your child it is a struggle and he or she needs help and encouragement. In fact the more 'normal' this behavior seems, the more upsetting it probably is for your child that he or she cannot do it as he or she may feel 'different' or 'freaky'. As well as motivating your child to have a go, the reward will boost his or her self-esteem by showing that you recognize the achievement he or she has made.

Observing others' behaviors

As we discussed in Part One, an important way that children learn to behave is by watching other people. Children can mimic how other people act, so it is important to keep an eye on your own behavior and take every opportunity to show your child a good example of how to deal with fears and worries. This does not mean covering up fears and worries. That can be hard to do, and children can be very perceptive. But it does mean expressing your fear, acknowledging that it is possibly 'a fear' rather than an actual threat, considering alternative ways of thinking about it, and not letting the fear get in your way.

Observing others' feelings

Children also learn about how to behave from how other people react to what *they* do in different situations. For example, Sarah's parents were very aware of Sarah's fear of spiders. Although neither of them was that keen on spiders themselves, they were very keen not to show any fear themselves in front of Sarah so that she wouldn't learn from them that spiders were scary. However, Sarah was on the lookout for any information that might suggest that spiders were to be feared (as we discussed in Chapter 2). When a spider was nearby, Sarah's parents couldn't help worrying that she might get upset. Sarah picked up on the subtle changes in her parents' expressions and interpreted these as more evidence that, indeed, spiders were something to avoid. At times anxious children can be very worrying, or frustrating. It is important to find ways to manage these feelings so that they do not interfere with the work that you are doing with your child. Chapter 12 focuses specifically on ways of managing your own anxiety to maximize the help you are giving your child.

Allowing independence

We have talked before about how anxious children often expect that they won't be able to cope in difficult situations and feel that they need to be protected. In order to overcome this your child needs to have the opportunity to develop independence, fight his or her own battles and make his or her own mistakes. Sometimes this can be very difficult, as you or others in your family might be inclined to step in and try to protect your child because you know that he or she may easily get upset. You can see, though, that by intervening in this way, the message to your child is that, 'I don't think you can cope', or 'You need my help.' You need to ask yourself whether you think that you are putting a lot of effort into trying to protect your child or controlling the world around him or her. Could your child be learning from you that you regard the world as a dangerous place and that you think that he or she can't manage on his or her own? If this is the case, then of course you won't want to just let your child suddenly deal with all the worries alone – you need to take a gradual (step by step) approach. This is the focus of the next chapter.

Have a go!

The table on the following pages (Responding to my child's anxious behavior) is for you to record how you get on using the strategies we have discussed to encourage your child to face his or her fears. Table 8.1 gives an example of the completed table, showing Jenny and her mum's record as they worked through Jenny's anxious thoughts about going to school. As usual, we would encourage you to keep a record whether you feel it worked or did not work. This way, over time you will be able to see a pattern and will have a clearer idea about which strategies work best with your child.

STEP 3: KEY POINTS

• Be on the lookout for your child 'having a go' (and not avoiding his or her fears).

• Praise and reward 'having a go'.

• Set your child a good example of how you manage your fears.

• Give your child clear messages that he or she can have a go and he or she can cope.

TABLE 8.1: RESPONDING TO MY CHILD'S ANXIOUS BEHAVIOR: JENNY'S EXAMPLE

Date	Behavior What did my child do?	Response What did I do?	Yes	No	Outcome What happened when I did this?
Example	Said she had a tummy ache before school	Cut out reassurance	✓		Jenny went to school (reluctantly)
		Asked about anxious thoughts	✓		Came home early (but it's a start).
		Helped her find alternative thoughts	✓		
		Gave clear and specific praise			
		Offered a reward	✓		
		Showed how I managed my own fears about the situation			
		Overcame my worries about her in this situation	✓		
		Stood back and allowed her to 'have a go'			

TABLE 8.2: RESPONDING TO MY CHILD'S ANXIOUS BEHAVIOR

Date	Behavior *What did my child do?*	Response *What did I do?*	Yes	No	Outcome *What happened when I did this?*
		Cut out reassurance			
		Asked about anxious thoughts			
		Helped him/her find alternative thoughts			
		Gave clear and specific praise			
		Offered a reward			
		Showed how I managed my own fears about the situation			
		Overcame my worries about him/in this situation			
		Stood back and allowed him/to 'have a go'			

TABLE 8.2: CONTINUED

Date	Behavior What did my child do?	Response What did I do?	Yes	No	Outcome What happened when I did this?
		Cut out reassurance			
		Asked about anxious thoughts			
		Helped him/her find alternative thoughts			
		Gave clear and specific praise			
		Offered a reward			
		Showed how I managed my own fears about the situation			
		Overcame my worries about him/her in this situation			
		Stood back and allowed him/her to 'have a go'			

An additional copy can be found in Appendix 2.

9

Step 4: A step-by-step approach to facing fears

Note: Read through all of Step 4 before trying to put any of the strategies into place.

One of the main ideas that we have talked about so far is that to become less scared or worried about something we need to 'face our fears' and find ways to cope with them.

Learning to face fears

As we have already discussed, fears won't go away unless we actually stand up to them. If we always avoid or run away from things that we are frightened of, we never find out whether they were really as bad as we thought or whether we could actually have coped with them. You will remember from the previous chapter that this is what happened to Jenny, who never put her hand up in class because she thought that if she asked her teacher a question her classmates would think she was stupid.

The main idea behind this chapter is that by facing fears gradually your child will find that he or she can tolerate more and more anxiety-provoking situations.

This may be because your child, like Jenny, discovers that her fears are unfounded. Or it may be that your child simply learns to put up with the feeling of fear without losing control. As we mentioned earlier, in addition to seeing possible danger, your anxious child may also feel that when confronted with danger he or she will not be able to cope. Facing fears can help your child overcome either or both of these ways of thinking.

A step-by-step approach

To Jenny, however, the idea of putting up her hand and speaking up in front of her class was terrifying. If we had just told her to get on and do this she would probably not have followed our advice, and may have been left feeling quite hopeless about becoming less anxious. One way to make it easier to face fears is slowly and gradually, step by step.

The idea of taking a gradual approach to doing something difficult is often familiar to children. For example, when we sometimes talk to children about how we should deal with a fear, they give us very good advice. The example below is taken from a conversation with a child in our clinic.

Therapist: 'The problem is that I really don't like dogs. They make me feel really scared. But my good friend has a very big dog and it barks a lot and I would really like to go and stay over at my friend's house. What do you think I should do? I could just go round anyway, but it is such a big dog I'm worried I'll be so scared that I'll have to leave. Do you think there is anything else I could do?'

Jack: 'Why don't you go and play with a little dog first?'

Therapist: 'That's such a good idea. I do have another friend who has a small dog that doesn't really bark very much; maybe I should visit them first. Then when I've got used to the small dog I might not feel so scared about the big one.'

Making a plan

Drawing up a clear step-by-step plan with your child will help you both focus on the goals you are aiming for. Again, making this task fun by being creative about how you present the plan and using characters and colours to decorate it will help your child to feel a part of the plan making. Create the structure for your plan first. For example, the plan could simply show a child moving up the steps of a ladder, or follow a rocket flying to the moon (stopping off at stars along the way) or a train going along a track (with the different steps marked as stations on the way to the final destination). Listen to what your child suggests and try to make the most of his or her interests. See the example provided below for some ideas.

There are five steps involved in making your step-by-step plan with your child as outlined in the box overleaf.

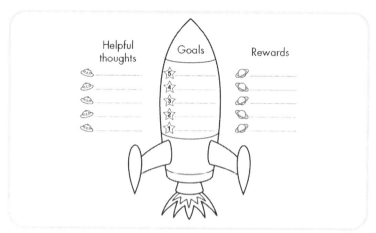

Figure 9.1 Example of an illustrated step-by-step plan

BOX 9.1 MAKING A STEP-BY-STEP PLAN

1 Identify your child's ultimate goal and ultimate reward.

2 List steps towards the ultimate goal.

3 Ask your child to rate the steps and put them in order from the least to the most scary.

4 Specify a reward to accompany each step.

5 Help your child consider helpful ways of thinking about the first step.

The ultimate goal

You and your child need to work out steps towards the ultimate goal. In order to do this you first need to be clear about what you are aiming for. You will find it hard to work on your step-by-step plan if you have a vague goal like 'Be less worried in class', as how will you really know when your child has achieved this? To keep it clear and simple the goal needs to be something you (or somebody) can *see* your child do. Here are some examples of ultimate goals.

Ultimate goals

Jenny: To ask my teacher a question in front of my class.

Tom: To sleep on my own in my own room all night, every night for a week.

Ben: To play upstairs on my computer for half an hour when everyone else is downstairs.

Sarah: To hold a live spider in my hand.

Manageable, realistic goals

As you can see these goals all describe behaviors (rather than feelings). Try to think about it in this way: if your child were no longer anxious about this particular situation, what would this mean he or she *could do?* Or, perhaps, it would be OK to be a little anxious, but what would he or she have to do to feel he or she has overcome the fear *enough?* For example, we could ask Jenny to stand up and speak in front of her whole school, but is that really necessary? Presumably, not speaking in front of her whole school is not causing Jenny a problem in her day-to-day life, whereas not being able to ask for help in class is. We need to keep the goals manageable.

The goals also need to be achievable and realistic. If Ben could play upstairs on his own for six hours, this would certainly be a test of whether he had overcome his fear, but it's unlikely that Ben would ever reach this goal, as during that time he's going to have to go to the toilet, and have something to eat, let alone get bored and lonely. Similarly, if we asked Tom to sleep on his own in his room every night for a month, but in fact his cousin came to stay over every weekend, it would be through no fault of Tom's that he hadn't achieved his goal. In summary, ultimate goals need to be clearly spelled-out behaviors that are achievable and realistic.

Two things that we have discussed in earlier chapters are going to be particularly important to help your child have a go at each step. One is coming up with helpful thoughts about the step. The other is having the incentive of a reward. We will come back to helpful thoughts shortly.

Rewards

Alongside the ultimate goal, you and your child also need to decide on the ultimate reward. For Step 3 (Chapter 8) you and your child came up with a list of possible rewards. Now is the time to go back to that list and find a reward that fits such a big achievement as reaching the ultimate goal. Write this down on your step plan alongside the ultimate goal.

BOX 9.2 ULTIMATE GOALS AND REWARDS

Jenny

Goal: to ask my teacher a question in front of my class.

Reward: go out for dinner with Mum.

Tom

Goal: to sleep on my own in my own room all night, every night for a week.

Reward: have four friends over for a sleepover.

Ben

Goal: to play upstairs on my computer for half an hour when everyone else is downstairs.

Reward: a day trip to a theme park.

Sarah

Goal: to hold a live spider in my hand.

Reward: go to the cinema with a friend.

Breaking it down into steps

Once you have your ultimate goal your task is to break this down into smaller, more manageable, steps. We find it is useful not to have more than about ten steps, so that your child is not overwhelmed and can see the end in sight. It can also be helpful to start with a step that your child already does some of the time. It will be easier to get the ball rolling with the step-by-step plan if your child can quickly and easily have a go at the first step. There is an example of Jenny's step-by-step plan on the facing page (when we first make a plan we need only to add the first 'helpful thought', as we explain later in the chapter).

As we can see, Jenny's steps each build up towards the ultimate goal of asking her teacher a question in front of the whole class. The steps are ordered from the lowest to the most anxiety-provoking for the child. It's not always obvious which situations your child will find the most frightening, so it is important to ask him or her what he or she thinks. So that you can work out how to order the steps, ask your child to rate how scared he or she would be while doing each step, on a scale like the one above.

BOX 9.3 JENNY'S STEP-BY-STEP PLAN

Ultimate goal: ask the teacher a question in front of the whole class.

Helpful thought:

Ultimate reward: dinner out.

Step 6: answer a question asked by the teacher (answer not planned) in front of the whole class.

Helpful thought:

Reward: go to the craft shop after school.

Step 5: answer a question asked by the teacher (planned in advance) in front of the whole class.

Helpful thought:

Reward: stop off on the way home at the coffee shop.

Step 4: ask the teacher a question in a small group.

Helpful thought:

Reward: make cakes with Mum.

Step 3: answer a question asked by the teacher (answer not planned) in a small group.

Helpful thought:

Reward: choose a favourite dinner.

Step 2: answer a question asked by the teacher (planned in advance) in a small group.

Helpful thought:

Reward: stop off on the way home for a magazine.

Step 1: ask the teacher a question after class has finished and classmates have gone.

Helpful thought: I have done this once before and nothing bad happened. My teacher told me what I wanted to know and that helped me do my homework.

Reward: praise from Mum and teacher.

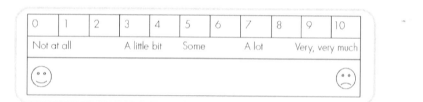

Figure 9.2 Worry scale

Use the table on the facing page to think of steps with your child, and ask your child to rate how anxious he or she would be about performing each step.

Once your child has done this you can add them in order – from the least to the most frightening – to your step-by-step plan, or you can use the table 9.2.

We find it is helpful to specify all the rewards for all the steps right from the start so that your child can clearly see what they are working towards and what they will gain along the way.

Helpful thoughts

In Chapters 6 and 7 you learned how to get your child to come up with more helpful, and less anxious, ways of thinking about his or her fears. These strategies can be now used to identify what your child is worried will happen when he or she has a go at the next step, and to help him or her work out if there are other (more helpful) ways of thinking about the step.

TABLE 9.1: HOW ANXIOUS DOES MY CHILD FEEL DOING EACH STEP?	
Steps to include in my child's step-by-step plan	How anxious does my child feel in this situation?

An additional copy can be found in Appendix 2.

There is no need to come up with helpful thoughts for all the steps at once; just focus on the step your child will be doing next, as it is likely that he or she will think quite differently about the ultimate goal once he or she has achieved some steps towards it. We have already seen, above, the helpful thought that Jenny came up with for her first step ('I have done this once before and nothing bad happened. My teacher told me what I wanted to know and that helped me do my homework'). On the following pages we can also see Sarah and Ben's step-by-step plans, with rewards for each step and a helpful thought for the first step they will encounter.

BOX 9.4 SARAH'S STEP-BY-STEP PLAN

Ultimate goal: hold a live spider in my hand.

Helpful thought:

Ultimate reward: go to the cinema with a friend.

Step 5: watch a live spider without a glass over it from a metre away or less, for at least a minute.

Helpful thought:

Reward: make cakes.

Step 4: watch a live spider under a glass for at least a minute.

Helpful thought:

Reward: play a board game with Dad.

Step 3: hold dead spider in hand.

Helpful thought:

Reward: a sweet from the jar.

Step 2: look at a dead spider under a magnifying glass.

Helpful thought:

Reward: praise from Mum and Dad.

Step 1: look at pictures of spiders in a book.

Helpful thought: these spiders can't hurt me.

Reward: praise from Mum and Dad.

TABLE 9.2: MY CHILD'S STEP-BY-STEP PLAN		
Goal	Helpful thought	Reward
10 (ultimate goal)		
9		
8		
7		
6		
5		
4		
3		
2		
1 (easiest step)		

An additional copy can be found in Appendix 2.

Putting it into practice

So far this chapter has been about how to put together a step-by-step plan. It is now time for your child to take the plunge and try the first step in the plan. As we mentioned earlier it can work well to start with a step that you know your child can achieve – for example, something that he or she may have done before once or twice. Even though he or she has done it before it is essential to give the child a lot of praise and encouragement so that he or she feels encouraged to keep going with the step-by-step plan.

Take your time

If the first step goes particularly well your child is likely to feel ready to rush on up through the steps to the ultimate goal. We would encourage you, however, to slow the pace down a little. It is important that your child feels truly confident at each step before moving on to the next step. Rushing ahead too quickly could lead your child to become very frightened by a step that he or she was not ready for, losing confidence and wanting to give up on the whole thing. Instead, we like to see each step being *repeated* until your child feels confident enough to continue. Your child may still feel scared or frightened by the step, but this fear should no longer be overwhelming. It should instead feel manageable in order to continue up the step-by-step plan. Of course you may not be able to give the same reward repeatedly, but be sure to continue to praise the achievement and, perhaps, offer a smaller token reward to acknowledge it.

BOX 9.5 BEN'S STEP-BY-STEP PLAN

Ultimate goal: to play upstairs on my computer for half an hour when Mum is downstairs.

Helpful thought:

Ultimate reward: a day trip to a theme park.

Step 7: to read or play in my bedroom for ten minutes with Mum anywhere downstairs.

Helpful thought:

Reward: go ice-skating.

Step 6: to read or play in my bedroom for five minutes with Mum in the kitchen.

Helpful thought:

Reward: go swimming.

Step 5: to read (or play) in my bedroom for five minutes with Mum at the bottom of the stairs.

Helpful thought:

Reward: have Charlie round to tea.

Step 4: to stay on the landing and read a book for five minutes with Mum downstairs in the kitchen. Helpful thought: Reward: a new book.

Step 3: to stay on the landing and read a book for five minutes with Mum downstairs.

Helpful thought:

Reward: choose a DVD to hire.

Step 2: to go to the top of the stairs and on to the landing with Mum at the bottom of the stairs.

Helpful thought:

Reward: two stickers.

Step 1: to go to the top of the stairs with Mum at the bottom of the stairs.

Helpful thought: I have been up the stairs before and Drog has never got me. Anyway, Mum will be able to keep an eye on me from the bottom of the stairs.

Reward: a sticker.

Getting stuck into a step

Before your child attempts each new step go back to the principles you used in Chapter 7 about helping your child to change how she or he thinks, and generate helpful thoughts. For example, Ben had successfully read and played in his bedroom for five minutes, while his mum waited for him (reading her own book) at the bottom of the stairs. He had his reward of having his friend Charlie round for tea and was excited about having a go at the next step. However, when the time came, Ben still felt very scared. Above is the conversation that Ben and his mum had for Ben to come up with a helpful thought that would help him attempt the next step. This conversation shows that Ben was still daunted by the next step, so his mum helped him break it down into smaller steps.

Mum: 'Ben, how do you feel about this next step?'

Ben: 'I don't want to do it.'

Mum: 'What is worrying you about it? What do you think might happen?'

Ben: 'If you go in the kitchen you won't be able to hear if something happens to me.'

Mum: 'What makes you think something will happen to you, Ben?

Ben: 'You know what!'

Mum: 'I think so. Is it Drog?'

Ben: 'Yes.'

Mum: 'Well, you've been doing so brilliantly sitting up the stairs this week. Have you seen Drog while you've been up there?'

Ben: 'No.'

Mum: 'What has happened while you've been up the stairs?'

Ben: 'Nothing. I just looked at my book.'

Mum: 'So if you went up now do you think Drog will come?'

Ben: 'We-ell, maybe not. But he might.'

Mum: 'OK. So it sounds like you think that Drog probably won't come and you'll probably just sit and look at your book with nothing happening. Let's write that thought down, as that sounds quite helpful to remember. But I know you're still a bit worried just in case Drog does come. So how about we make this a smaller step? Why don't I go away from the bottom of the stairs, but not as far as the kitchen just yet?'

Ben: 'Yes, you could just go into the living room.'

Mum: 'OK. Good idea. I'll do that.'

Safety behaviors

Safety behaviors are things that children might do to make themselves feel safe enough to have a go at facing a fear. These can be things like making sure they are not alone, that they have a particular object with them or that they are hidden in some way. The potential problem with safety behaviors is that they can prevent a child learning that they can cope in a situation because they believe they managed it only because of the safety behavior. Be on the lookout for safety behaviors that your child might adopt. Although, for example, having a favourite toy in a pocket might help your child to face a fear the first time, make sure that he or she does not become reliant on this prop. For example, the next step could be to repeat the same step without the toy, in return for an even greater reward.

When the step does not go well

If your child has a go at the step but it doesn't go as well as you'd both hoped, it is still important to praise your child for having had a go and trying to face the fear. It may just have been a bad day, in which case encourage your child not to give up but to try again as soon as possible. Or it may be that some more planning is needed. For example, Jenny's step-by-step plan included her teacher asking her a question that they had planned in advance. Clearly some forward planning would be needed here, so Jenny's mum made an appointment to see the teacher to tell her about the plan that she and Jenny were following. Jenny's mum took the opportunity to tell the teacher about the different methods that she had been using, and particularly what she found had helped Jenny the most. Jenny's teacher was happy to get involved with the plan, and agreed to meet Jenny before the start of class to decide together what question she would ask Jenny and what answer Jenny should give. Once she was aware of what Jenny and her mother were trying to do the teacher was also able to be on the lookout for any signs of progress that Jenny made in terms of speaking up in class, and made sure to give Jenny a wink or a smile. As well as teachers, try to get on board anyone who may be able to help and encourage your child, for example, family members, club leaders and friends. The more praise and support your child receives the better he or she will feel about his or her achievements.

STEP 4: KEY POINTS

- Avoidance keeps the fear going.

- Help your child to face fears gradually.

- Draw up a step-by-step plan with your child.

- Help your child come up with helpful thoughts about the next step he or she faces.

- Praise and reward your child's attempts at each step.

- If a step is too much too soon, break it down into smaller steps.

- Practise, practise, practise.

10

Step 5: Problem solving

Note: Read through all of Step 5 before trying to put any of the strategies into place.

Up to now the emphasis has been on helping your child to think about things in a less anxious way, to see the world as less scary, and to have a go and face his or her fears. Sometimes, however, your child may have good reason for seeing a particular situation as frightening. For example, a child who is being bullied would understandably feel nervous about attending school. Although this is a genuinely difficult experience, you might be able to imagine this same thing happening to some children that you know and their not getting quite so anxious as a result. The thing that is likely to make the difference to how anxious a child gets is his or her own sense of how able he or she is to sort out the problem. As we have said in earlier chapters, children who are more anxious are more likely to think that they won't be able to cope with a situation and come up with solutions which get them out of that situation as quickly as possible (rather than coming up with a solution that will stop this problem from happening again). We want to help your child to be able to recognize when there is a problem and to feel confident about getting that problem solved.

When problem solving is needed

Sometimes problems may emerge while you are investigating anxious thoughts with your child. For example, if your child feared being bullied you would probably ask, 'Has anything like that happened to you before?' If you then discovered that it had, and was still happening, then this would clearly require positive action. By using problem solving you can work with your child to decide what is the best thing to do. (For more information on dealing with bullying see Chapter 18.) Problem solving may also be useful if your child reaches a step on the step-by-step plan that requires some organizing in advance. For example, one of Sarah's steps was to look at a dead spider under a magnifying glass, but Sarah had neither a dead spider nor a magnifying glass! Rather than use this as an opportunity to avoid doing the step, Sarah and her father used problem solving to work out what they could do to overcome this difficulty.

Another situation in which problem solving can be useful is when you and your child have gone through the methods described in Chapter 7 to consider how your child is thinking about a feared situation, and your child has concluded that the feared situation is not very likely, but it still *is* apossibility. You will remember from Chapter 8 that as well as interpreting situations as threatening, anxious children also tend to see themselves as being unable to deal with any threat that they might come across. Problem solving can be useful to help your child work out either how to deal with a problem that does arise (as above) or how to take control and prevent a problem arising.

Becoming an independent problem solver

When a child is very anxious it can be very tempting to try to solve problems for him or her. After all, as parents, we want to do all that we can to stop our children from becoming upset. But if your child is going to feel confident that problems can be solved, whether you are there or not, then he or she needs to learn how to solve problems for himor herself. This doesn't mean that your child can't ask others for help. Asking for help can be a good strategy for solving many problems (and is often essential, for example, in a bullying situation), but it is your child's responsibility to consider this solution among other possibilities and to come to a decision about the best way forward.

Step-by-step problem solving

Once again there is a series of steps involved in becoming an independent and effective problem solver. The steps that we describe may seem familiar to you, as many adults will use these steps automatically when they are faced with a problem. The steps are: (i) being clear about what the problem is; (ii) thinking of as many solutions as possible; and (iii) weighing up the pros and cons of each solution to decide which will be the best. Following these steps will help your child to be clear about what he or she needs to do to develop this new skill. Eventually the steps will become second nature to you and your child, and it may not be necessary to sit and work through them all one by one, but to get to this stage we would encourage you to stick with the steps until solving problems in this way becomes a habit.

At the end of this chapter you will find some problem-solving tables to fill out, which will guide you and your child through the steps. We would urge you to use the tables and keep a written record of your child's attempts at problem solving, because (i) having it written in front of you keeps it simple, as there is less to remember; (ii) it makes the process that you are working through thoroughly clear to your child; and (iii) should the same problem happen again in the future your child can look back at the table to see what can be done.

What is the problem?

It seems obvious, but the first step is to find out what the problem is. The only way to be completely clear about this is for your child to describe the problem to you. You cannot assume that you know what it is.

When your child has told you then use your own words to check that you have understood. Whether you think this is a genuine cause for concern or not, it is clearly worrying your child, so it deserves your understanding, but you should keep it quite matter of fact. We want to get across to your child, that, yes, you can see that he or she is worried and that there is a problem to be solved. So how is it going to be solved?

On the facing page is an example of a conversation that Jenny and her mother had the night before a supply teacher was coming in to the classroom.

Weird and wonderful solutions

Your child may find it difficult to come up with solutions to problems; after all, maybe until now he or she has avoided dealing with problems. Or maybe problems have all been sorted out for him or her. Whatever the reason, this step is all about helping your child to get into the habit of finding solutions. At this point you shouldn't care what the solutions are, or even if they would work, you just want solutions and lots of them! Just coming up with a solution – any solution – deserves praise, and every idea deserves to be taken seriously. The fact that your child is having a go at thinking of ways to overcome problems and anxiety is a positive and important step!

If your child really struggles to come up with any solutions then you may need to give gentle prompts. But, as before, try to ask questions rather than making solutions. For example, 'What would someone else do in this situation?', 'When this happened before, can you remember what you did then?', or if more is needed, 'I know someone who had this problem and they did..., do you think you could do anything like that?'

Mum: 'Jenny, you have seemed much happier about going to school recently, but now you are saying you don't want to go. Is something bothering you?'

Jenny: 'We've got a supply teacher coming in tomorrow.'

Mum: 'And what worries you about that?'

Jenny: 'He might be someone we haven't had before so he won't know that I find maths really difficult and might get cross if I can't answer a question.'

Mum: 'I see – so you are worried that he'll think that if you got a question wrong it must be because you weren't paying attention or something, rather than it being because you found the question difficult?'

Jenny: 'Yes.'

Mum: 'This sounds like a situation we talked about before. I remember you came up with lots of other possible things that might happen and in the end you thought it might not turn out as badly as you feared.'

Jenny: 'I know that the teacher might not ask me a question, and even if he did I might not get it wrong, and even if I did get it wrong he might not think I'm stupid. But I still can't help thinking, "What if that *does* happen?"'

Mum: 'Hmm, that does sound like a tricky situation. Let's have a think and see if we can come up with any things you could do to sort it out.'

On the next page is the conversation that Jenny and her mother had to try to think of as many solutions as they could to sort out the problem of Jenny having a supply teacher who would not know that she struggled in maths.

Jenny: 'I don't know what I can do about it – except stay home!' (Face lights up!)

Mum: 'OK. That's one solution. Well done. What other solutions can we come up with?'

Jenny: 'Send a snowstorm to my school so it can't open tomorrow.'

Mum: 'Yes. Good [laughing]. Anything else you could do?'

Jenny: 'I don't know.'

Mum: 'What about your friend Jane? She struggles a bit with English, doesn't she? What does she do when there is a supply teacher?'

Jenny: 'She has a Statement, so all the teachers will know that she needs help.'

Mum: 'OK. So making sure the teacher knows in advance might help. How could we do that?'

Jenny: 'You could write a note.'

Mum: 'That's a good idea. Or is there anything you could do? Like at the beginning of the lesson?'

Jenny: 'I could tell the teacher.'

Mum: 'Great. Another really good idea. Well done.'

Which is the best solution?

Your child needs to learn how to choose which is going to be the best solution to try. In order to do that he or she needs to consider (i) what would happen (in the long and short term); and (ii) how practical (or doable) the solution is. As you are taking all the solutions your child has come up with seriously, go through all the ideas one by one (even the seemingly silly ones) to find out what would happen and whether that solution would be doable. The box on the facing page gives some example questions to get your child thinking about the consequences of each solution.

BOX 10.1 WHICH IS THE BEST SOLUTION?

Example questions to ask:

'What would happen if you did...?'

'What would happen in the end?'

'Would it make any difference to what would happen in the future or if this problem came up again?'

'How would that change how you would feel if this problem came up again?'

Again, your child may not be used to thinking in this way. In this case you may need to prompt your child gently again. As before, try to stick to asking questions rather than giving answers, to help your child think about this for him- or herself. You will see an example of this in the conversation between Jenny and her mum below.

Mum: 'We've got lots of different ideas to choose from. So let's think about what would happen if you did each of these things. The first thing was "stay at home". So what would happen if you stayed home?'

Jenny: 'I wouldn't be in the class so the teacher couldn't ask me a question.'

Mum: 'That's true. What else would happen? What would happen in the long term?'

Jenny: 'Nothing.'

Mum: 'Do you think that if you missed school every time there was a supply teacher anyone might notice?'

Jenny: 'Yes – well you might. And my class teacher would.'

Mum: 'And then what would happen?'

Jenny: 'I'd get into trouble.'

Mum: 'Hmm, maybe. And how would you feel next time you had a supply teacher? Would you feel less worried?'

Jenny: 'No. I'd probably feel the same.'

Mum: 'OK. Well done. Let's jot that down ... Now, let's look at the next one: "send a snowstorm". What would happen if you chose that one?'

Jenny: 'The whole school would get covered in snow and all the lessons would be cancelled.'

Mum: 'OK. And what would happen after that?'

Jenny: 'When all the snow had melted we'd all go back in but I would have missed tomorrow's lesson.'

Mum: 'And what would you do next time you had a supply teacher?'

Jenny: 'I'd probably still be worried so I'd have to send the snow again!'

> Mum: 'Wow. That all sounds quite amazing. How about getting me to write a note to the supply teacher. What would happen if you did that?'

Jenny's responses to her mother's questions about the other solutions are all shown in the example table, at the end of this chapter.

Once your child has considered the possible outcomes he or she needs to think about which solution is actually going to be possible to carry out. Some example questions are given in the box below.

BOX 10.2 FINDING THE BEST SOLUTION

Example questions to ask:

'Is this solution possible?'

'So would you be able to try this solution?'

'Is there anything that would make this solution difficult to do?'

With all this information, your child can then decide how good each solution is. By giving a number to each solution it is then easy to compare the different solutions and choose the best ones. Your child should by now be familiar with using a rating scale. Use the rating scale below to rate how good each solution is.

Figure 10.1 Rating scale

As in all of the exercises, try to hold back your judgment and allow your child to decide how good each solution is for him- or herself. After all, if you decide that it is great, but your child has reservations, then he or she is not going to be very motivated to give this solution a try.

Make a decision and have a go!

Once the possible solutions have been rated, taking into account the consequences and the practicalities, it will be easy to see which will be the best one to try. Before he or she gets started, check that your child has everything needed to put the plan into action. Have a practice run or try role-playing first. Does your child need to get anyone else involved?

How did it go?

After your child has had a go you need to check how he or she got on. If the plan of action did not work out as well as your child had hoped, help him or her to think about whether there is anything that could be done differently next time. Or is it worth trying another one of the solutions that he or she came up with? But do remember, no matter how it went, your child deserves praise for having a go at overcoming a problem.

What is the problem?	List all the possible solutions	What would happen if I chose this solution?	Is this plan doable? Yes/No	How good is this plan? Rate 0–10	What happened?
Supply teacher at school tomorrow will not know I find maths hard and will get cross with me because he will think I was not paying attention	1. Stay home.	1. I wouldn't get asked any questions. I would get in trouble with teacher/Mum. I'd still be worried about supply teachers.	Yes	2	
	2. Send a snowstorm to school.	2. Lessons would be cancelled. I'd still be worried about supply teachers.	No	5	
	3. Mum to write a note to the teacher	3. I'd go to the class. If I didn't know an answer the teacher would understand and not get me cross. Next time we could do the same thing and I probably wouldn't worry so much about it but I would need Mum to sort it out for me. This could be a problem if I don't know in advance that there'll be a supply teacher	Yes	7	
	4. Jenny to speak to the teacher before class	4. I'd go to the class. I'd feel a bit embarrassed talking to the teacher. If I didn't know an answer the teacher would understand and not get me cross. Next time, I could do the same thing and I probably wouldn't worry so much about it	Yes	8	I went in early and told the teacher that I find maths hard. He still did ask a question, but I could answer it

Caption: TABLE 10.1: PROBLEM SOLVING: JENNY'S EXAMPLE

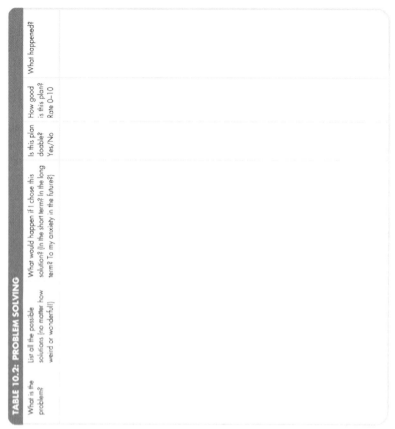

An additional copy can be found in Appendix 2.

STEP 5: KEY POINTS

• Help your child to define the problem clearly.

• Encourage your child to come up with as many solutions as possible.

• Ask your child questions to get him or her thinking about the consequences of each solution and how practical it is.

• Ask your child to rate each solution and choose which is the best.

- Recognize the step your child has made towards becoming an independent problem solver.

11

Additional Principles 1: Overcoming worry

Note: Read through the whole of this chapter before starting to put the strategies into place. This chapter also requires you to have read Chapter 5.

Worry will be something that is very familiar to you, not just because your child may be a worrier, but because worry is something that everybody does at some time. Worrisome thoughts go round and round in our heads, causing more anxiety, and making us feel that there are no solutions, just more problems. At times, however, it can seem as if worry has taken over. Worries may have started to feel uncontrollable to your child and, even if he or she is briefly distracted, his or her mind may seem to wander back to the worry. In the end, a large portion of your child's day may be spent worrying. The strategies that we describe in this chapter focus on the two main features of worry: (i) that it spirals out of control; and (ii) that it reaches no resolution. To take control of worry your child needs to be able to (i) put a limit on the time spent worrying; and (ii) turn 'worry' into 'finding solutions'.

Putting a limit on worry

'Worry time'

If your child seems to be spending a lot of the day worrying, or coming to you repeatedly with worries, then it is a good idea to set aside a 'worry time'. This is a fixed amount of time (limit it to about half an hour) when you and your child will discuss any worries that have come up during the day. The worry time needs to be at a time when both you and your child are able to think; so, for example, when your child is not either very tired or very hungry, and you are not trying to get a million other things done. Choose a time when you and your child can sit and talk together without interruptions.

'Worry list'

Keep a record of worries somewhere safe so that you or your child can add to it with any worries that come up between worry times. So, if a worry comes up during the day, make a note of it and carry on with what you were doing – this may feel harsh on your child, but as long as your child sees that 'worry time' happens he or she will soon be confident that the worry is not being forgotten or dismissed. Your child may take to this more easily if you can make the record special in some way – for example, use a special book, and perhaps you and your child could decorate it or stick on pictures of characters or celebrities that he or she likes. Alternatively, you can make and decorate a posting box that your child can post worries into throughout the day.

Below, we will talk about what happens during worry time, but it is also worth noting that for many children just this act of saving worries until later can be very helpful. Children (and adults) can feel that by worrying they are doing something and if they don't worry things will get worse. Saving worries for later will show your child that nothing disastrous happens when they don't worry. Instead, through keeping a note of them, the worries can start to seem repetitive or even boring ('not that one again!') – and as a result, much easier to ignore.

Cut out reassurance

Between worry times it may be tempting to offer your child some kind of reassurance that he or she doesn't need to worry. Of course, this is a natural response, but you must resist. Think back to all the times you have reassured your child and said, 'Don't worry.' Did that put an end to all the worrying? We assume that in most cases the answer will be 'No'. In fact it is often the case that when we are told not to think about something, we end up thinking about it more!

Try this yourself. Imagine now a big brown bear sitting on your living room floor eating a jar of honey. Now – don't think about it!

When you were told not to think about it did the image just come straight back into your head? For the majority of people the answer would be yes. So trying to not think about something is not helpful. In addition, as we discussed in Chapter 8, rather than giving your child reassurance, what you are aiming for is your child to be able to feel more in control of worries him- or herself, even when you are not close by.

Distraction

Instead of reassurance (once you have made a note of the worry to discuss later) you may need to help your child to distract him- or herself, to take his or her mind off the worry. Try to create a game that will use your child's full concentration. For example, if you are in the car, take a bet on how many red cars you will see before you reach your destination and get your child to count, or look at cars around you and try to make words using the letters from their number plates. If you are at home, find your child a job that will engross him or her and that he or she will enjoy.

Turning 'worry' into 'finding solutions'

There is no harm at all in your child thinking or talking about problems; in fact it is an important thing to do. But the thinking needs to be constructive and this is where you come in. Our tips for this are based on the methods that were discussed in Chapters 6, 7 and 10, to help your child to think differently about the worry if he or she is overestimating the chance of bad things happening, or to come up with solutions to problems. Sometimes you may find it useful to combine the methods from these chapters. For example, your child may acknowledge that there is only a slight chance of the bad thing happening, but even so it is still very frightening to think that it could happen at all. In this case, it may be useful to help your child think about what he or she could do in the event that it did happen (even though it may not be very likely).

Although we have talked mostly about Ben's fear of Drog the monster, Ben was also described by his parents as 'a real worrier'. He worried about many different things including war, terrorism and 'bad people'. Ben's parents had planned a trip to the city and he was looking forward to many aspects of it, but he could not help worrying about a bomb going off when they were travelling by public transport. This worry kept coming back to him. Even when he was doing something completely different it would just pop into his head and he would find it difficult to stop thinking about it. Ben's parents found it difficult to know how to respond to this worry, as it was true that terrible events like the ones Ben feared do happen sometimes, and Ben had seen reports about them on the news. No matter how much they wished it were true they could not honestly promise Ben that this would never happen. When Ben mentioned his worry, his dad made a note of it and asked Ben to post it into his worry box. They had the following conversation later on at worry time.

Dad: 'So Ben, we wrote down that you were worried about a bomb going off when we are on the bus on Saturday. What makes you think that will happen?'

Ben: 'I saw it on the news.'

Dad: 'You're right, that has happened before. It was a horrible thing to happen.'

Ben: 'Yes, I saw all these people with blood all over them.'

Dad: 'Yes, there were people hurt on that news report. Did you see any other people on the report who hadn't been hurt?'

Ben: 'Well, there were all the people who saw it who were talking about it.'

Dad: 'And do you think those people had been on a bus before then?'

Ben: 'Yes, they were all talking about how they always got that bus to work.'

Dad: 'Do you remember if we've been on a bus before when we've gone in to the city?'

Ben: 'Yes, we went on that double-decker bus when we went to the museum.'

Dad: 'Did anything happen that time?'

Ben: 'No. We just bought a ticket from the driver and then sat on the top so we could see out.'

Dad: 'That's right. We got a really good view didn't we? So it sounds like you're saying that although there was a bomb on one bus that we saw on the news, most of the time nothing happens like that. And when it does happen not everyone gets hurt.'

Ben: 'Yes, but what if it did happen?'

Dad: 'Well, what do you think? What do you think we could do?'

Ben: 'Maybe if we sat near the door we'd be able to get off quickly if anything did happen.'

Dad: 'Yes, we could do that. Anything else we could do?'

Ben: 'If there was flying glass like on the TV, then we could duck down behind our seat so it doesn't get us.'

Dad: 'That's a very good idea. Is there anything else?'

Ben: 'We could call 999 on your mobile phone so an ambulance comes straight away.'

> Dad: 'Yes. That's really good, too. So we think it's most likely that a bomb won't go off, but it sounds like we have a plan just in case it does. Right?'

Accepting uncertainty

Helpful thoughts

As we can see in the above example, sometimes we cannot be sure that the situation we fear is not going to happen. This is often the case for general worries about death, war, disaster or the health of our planet. Your child can go a long way by considering the likelihood of these events and having a plan of action should the worst occur. However, there also comes a point where it is necessary to accept that sometimes we can't know for sure what is going to happen. At these times, your child has to learn to live with the fact that there are some events over which we may have no control. At these times the idea of a 'helpful thought' is useful. The fear may be realistic, but how 'helpful' is it in helping your child get on and enjoy their life? Like most children at some time, among Tom's worries was the fear that both his parents would die and he would be left alone. From working through the strategies in Chapters 6, 7 and 10 in particular, Tom's parents helped him to come to the following conclusions.

BOX 11.1 TOM'S THOUGHTS ABOUT HIS PARENTS DYING

'Both my parents are fit and well so the chances of them dying soon from being ill are quite low, but there is always the possibility that they could be in an accident or something. If that happened I'd go and live with Aunt Sue. I'd always miss my parents a lot but Aunt Sue would look after me until I'm a grown up and can look after myself. Thinking about my parents dying doesn't stop it from happening and it makes me feel miserable and want to stay in all the time. So, seeing as they are alive, I should make the most of it and get out and do things and enjoy myself.'

Unsurprisingly, Tom did not immediately feel better after coming to these conclusions. He still felt very sad about the fact that his parents could (and would at some point) die. Tom's parents encouraged him to let them know when it worried him again and each time it was put on the day's worry list. At worry time, they could then read again the conclusions that he had come to before and discuss any other worries he had that related to his parents dying. It was a difficult subject for Tom's parents, as they could not help Tom come to any easy answers. Importantly, they managed to get a balance by being understanding of Tom's worries but also keeping a focus on what could be done to take control of this worry. Also, as it was a topic that could lead to more and more questions and be talked about for hours, it was essential for Tom's parents to keep to their limit of half an hour's worry time each day. After all, the worry could always be carried over to the next day's worry time if it came up for Tom again after worry time.

Focus on 'here and now'

At times of uncertainty you can assist your child by helping him or her to stay 'in the here and now' – in other words, to think about and concentrate fully on what is happening right now, not what has just happened, or what happened last week, or what is going to happen next Friday. This is another one of those things that sounds simple, but in fact can really be quite difficult. If you think about it, how often are you completely focused on what you are doing? Or are you at the same time thinking about when the car is due for an MOT, when the house insurance needs to be paid, or when you're going to get time to do the ironing? If you were able to think about times when you were completely focused on the whole experience of what you were doing it may well have been playing a sport or some other kind of game, or a puzzle perhaps. There is no doubt that one reason why people find these kinds of activities relaxing is because they enable us to take time out of our busy lives to just focus on what we are doing there and then.

Try to take opportunities to be an example to your child of 'being in the here and now' – when you are doing something then *really do it.* Even if it is just the washing-up, concentrate on how it feels, what you can smell, what you can see. Also, encourage your child to do the same. When he or she is helping you make cakes don't ask what he or she would like for dinner tonight and what you should do at the weekend, but ask about the feel of the mixture, the smell, how it looks. If you feel uncertain about the benefits of doing this give it a try for yourself first, but do give it a proper try. Remember: like any skill it takes time and practise to get it right.

Children naturally gravitate towards the kinds of leisure and sporting activities mentioned above, which allow them to free their minds from fears and worries and just focus on the here and now. Be on the lookout for activities that engage your child in this way and encourage him or her. For children to achieve in life, it is not all about academic or social success. They also need to have good, useful and effective ways of switching off and recharging their batteries. Worrying is not switching off, although trampolining may well be!

OVERCOMING WORRY: KEY POINTS

- Set a designated 'worry time' with your child.

- Keep a 'worry list'.

- Hold back reassurance. Use distraction if required.

- Discover, with your child, what makes him or her hold a worrying thought.

- Help your child consider other points of view and generate 'helpful thoughts'.

- Work through the problem-solving steps with your child to find solutions.

- Look out for activities in which your child is 'in the here and now', and encourage these.

12

Additional Principles 2: Managing your own anxiety

Note: Read through the whole of this chapter before starting to put the strategies into place. This chapter also requires you to have read Chapter 5.

As we discussed in Chapter 3, there are likely to be several factors that have led to your child becoming anxious. It doesn't really matter what originally *caused* your child to be anxious. What does matter, however, are any factors that may be keeping the anxiety going, or getting in the way of you and your child overcoming his or her anxiety.

As we said at the beginning of Part Two, parents of children who are anxious are often themselves highly anxious. When anxious children with anxious parents receive treatment for their anxiety, they do much better if the parents' anxiety is treated first. There are two main reasons for this. First, if you are less anxious your child will start to learn other ways of thinking and behaving from you. Second, if you are less anxious you are likely to find it less difficult to follow this program.

If you are an anxious person yourself, by making a concerted effort to overcome this you will not only be helping yourself but you will also be helping your anxious child. In this chapter we will first talk about methods of tackling your own anxiety. For more extensive advice on overcoming your own anxiety problems you may find it useful to read other titles in this series (see Appendix 1). We will then discuss specific ways in which your own anxiety may impact upon your attempts to help your child and how to overcome these.

Overcoming your own fears and worries

As we discussed earlier, experiencing anxiety is a normal thing – it happens to everyone. The point at which it becomes a problem, however, is when it starts getting in the way of your life – your work, your friendships, your family and your parenting. If you recognize that anxiety is stopping you from doing things you would like to be doing then it is important to address your fears and worries.

Use the box below to write a list of fears and worries that you feel interfere with your life.

BOX 12.1 MY OWN FEARS AND WORRIES

1 _____

2 _____

3 _____

4 _____

5 _____

6 _____

The strategies that have been discussed in this book are not used exclusively with children or young people, but are very similar to strategies that adults can use. Although we do recommend a number of books aimed at adults to help them overcome anxiety or other difficulties with mood or feelings, there is no reason why you cannot use the strategies and skills that you have learned in this book yourself. To recap, the box on the facing page summarizes the main strategies we have focused on.

By overcoming your own anxiety you will be making it much easier for both yourself and your child when it comes to helping him or her overcome anxiety. We will now turn to some of the specific ways in which you being less anxious will encourage your child's progress.

Encouraging helpful thinking

In Chapter 7 you learned how to get your child to discover new, 'helpful', ways of thinking about situations that he or she feared. As we discussed in that section, anxious children and anxious adults both tend to think about things in a similar way: seeing situations as threatening, feeling unable to cope with that threat, and anticipating that they will become really distressed. In Chapter 3 we talked about how children can learn from watching others. Seeing a parent think about the world in this way may encourage a child to do the same.

On the other hand, if a parent can set an example for a child of how to think about things in a helpful way this will help the child learn this new way of seeing the world. This is quite different from a parent trying to cover up fears. Children often say that they feel like they are the only one that feels the way they do, they feel like they are a 'freak' for feeling scared all the time. Often they are not aware that *everyone* has fears and that *everyone* feels scared sometimes. Rather than hiding all your fears from your child it is important to show that having fears is normal and that there are ways of dealing with them so that they don't take over your life.

BOX 12.2 OVERCOMING YOUR OWN ANXIETY

1 Overcoming your anxious thoughts

How are you thinking about situations and people that you come across? Are you expecting the worst? Seeing danger all around you? Would other people think about these situations differently? What is the evidence to support how you are thinking? Is there any evidence to suggest you could think differently?

On the next page you will find a similar chart to the one you used with your child in Chapter 7. This time try out the chart to consider one of your own fears or worries. First, of course, you need to get a clear idea of what your worry is. Then you can consider the evidence for or against your worry. On the basis of this do there seem to be other ways of thinking about this situation?

2 Overcoming avoidant behavior

Are you keeping away from the things that scare or worry you? How can you come to face the fear gradually? Make your own step-by-step plan. Reward yourself for your progress and encourage others to reward you, too.

3 Overcoming problems

Do you feel paralyzed when confronted with a problem? Instead, try to focus on solutions. What are all the possible things you could do (no matter how silly)? What would happen if you did these things? What will be the best solution? Give it a try and see how it goes.

4 Overcoming worry

Do your worries spiral out of control? Put a limit on worrying. Allocate a set time to your worries, and use this time to find solutions. At other times practise keeping focused on the 'here and now'.

TABLE 12.1: HELPING MYSELF WITH UNHELPFUL THOUGHTS

What is happening?	What am I thinking?	Evidence and alternatives	What happened in the end?
	Why are you worried? What do you think will happen? What is it about [this fear] that is making you worried?	What makes you think that [this fear] will happen? Has that ever happened to you before? Have you ever seen that happen to someone else? How likely is it that [this fear] will happen? Can you imagine that anything else could happen? If [this fear] did happen, could there be any other reasons for it? What would you think was happening if someone else was in the same boat? What would someone else think if they were in this situation? How could you test this out?	What did you think? What did you do? How did you feel?

An additional copy can be found in Appendix 2.

The way that fears are talked about and responded to makes a big difference to whether children adopt the fear for themselves. For example, Jenny was perfectly aware that her mother had a fear of cats. However, Jenny's mum had never stopped Jenny stroking cats or playing with cats that belonged to other people. Jenny's mum would say to her, 'It's just me that doesn't like cats, a lot of people love them.' Because Jenny had been able to have her own positive experiences with cats, despite her mother's fear, Jenny did not share the fear. From her mum letting her know that different people felt differently about cats and from having the opportunity to play with cats, she did not think of her mum's fear as a sign that 'cats are scary and dangerous', instead she thought of it as 'just Mum's funny worry'. How you discuss your fears or worries with your child is, therefore, very important. In particular, they need to be talked about as 'just' fears or worries rather than as facts. To help you think about your fears and whether they are 'just' fears as opposed to facts, try out for yourself the strategies we discussed in Chapters 6 and 7.

Of the fears and worries that you are challenging, you may want to select one that is appropriate to share with your child (for example, a fear of cats rather than something of an adult nature such as money or relationships worries). Your child may be able to help you go through the chart, asking you the questions; this could help him or her to feel more and more of an expert when it comes to 'helpful thinking'.

Worries about your child

Having a child is worrying. Having an anxious child is more worrying! Having an anxious child when you are already an anxious person yourself – well, it's clearly not going to be easy. It is normal to worry about your child, but as with all worries if they are getting in the way of you parenting your child in the manner that you would like to, then these worries need tackling. If your child is aware of the extent that you worry about them he or she will not want to be open with you about his or her own worries for fear of upsetting you further. You need to be able to show your child that you can deal with worry.

What do you expect of your child?

As we have said, anxious children do present a worry to their parents, but if a parent already tends to be very anxious this is likely to be amplified. We have found that parents who think in an anxious way tend to expect their child to see the world in a similar way. How parents think about their child will, of course, influence how they behave with their child.

If you think your child is going to get very upset, of course you are going to want to do what you can to stop this from happening. You may want to remove him or her from the situation and provide reassurance that he or she will be all right. On the other hand you may expect that he or she is going to make a big fuss and then feel annoyed or irritated and become snappy or cross with your child. Although both of these reactions are completely understandable given how you are expecting your child to react, they are likely to get in the way of the work you are doing to help your child overcome his or her fears, worries and anxiety.

Jenny's mum, like Jenny, often became very anxious about what other people thought of her. She found it extremely difficult, therefore, when

Jenny started to make a fuss about going into school at the school gates. It seemed to her that all the other children were going in just fine, it was just her child making a fuss, and all the other parents must be watching and thinking she was a useless parent. Now, as they approached the school gates Jenny's mum started to feel her fear that Jenny was going to make a scene creep up on her. She found it difficult to concentrate on her plan of how she was going to manage Jenny's fear, as she was getting overwhelmed by her own anxiety. When Jenny spoke to her she couldn't help snapping back at her. She could see that this was not helping Jenny feel positively about going into school.

Anxious signals

Giving negative information

Both your own worries and your worries about your child can sometimes 'leak out', and be visible to others. You need to be on the lookout for subtle expressions of anxiety when you are with your child. Ask a friend, partner or relative to watch you when you encounter a stressful situation with your child. Can they help you spot whether your anxious feelings are showing themselves and getting in the way of you helping your child? For example, despite maintaining a calm manner, do you cross the road whenever a dog approaches? Or, despite being hospitable to your new neighbours, would you still express relief when they have gone home? These are examples of ways we unwittingly display signs of our own anxiety.

We talked earlier, in relation to Chapter 8 (encouraging independence and 'having a go'), about Sarah's parents, who were really worried that Sarah might become upset and not be able to cope if she saw a spider. Sarah picked up on the little changes in her parents' expressions when they spotted a spider and interpreted these as more evidence that spiders were, indeed, something to be feared. What we expect our children to fear and how we expect them to cope with threat is influenced by how we, ourselves, think about threat. Furthermore, our expectations of our children are likely to influence how we behave around them (particularly at times of fear or stress) and this may influence how our children actually cope themselves. This creates another vicious cycle.

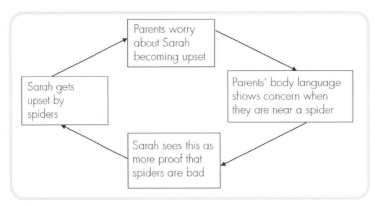

Figure 12.1 How expectations affect how children think and feel

Both Jenny's mum and Sarah's mum and dad sat down and completed charts to see if there was a different way that they could think about their children and their fears. What they came up with is shown on the following pages.

Giving positive information

Being positive about your child's attempts at facing his or her fears can be more difficult for a parent who feels anxious. For example, mothers who feel very anxious in social situations tend to look concerned when their child interacts with a friendly stranger. Children pick this up and become more worried in the future by the presence of a stranger. Feeling anxious when your child is in a situation that would scare you may relate to what you are expecting to happen to your child or how you are expecting him or her to feel, as we discussed above. It is important to recognize these thoughts and expectations so that they don't get in the way of your being able to support your child in facing fears in a fun and relaxed way. Use a thought record to challenge thoughts that are making it hard to feel truly positive about your child facing their fears.

162

TABLE 12.2: HELPING MYSELF WITH UNHELPFUL THOUGHTS: MUM'S WORRIES ABOUT JENNY

What is happening?	What am I thinking?	Evidence and alternatives	What happened in the end?
Approaching the school gates with Jenny to drop her off	**Why are you worried?** Jenny is not going to want to go to school. **What is it about this situation that is making you worried?** She'll kick and cry and cry. Everyone will look at me and think I'm a terrible parent.	**Has that ever happened to you before?** Yes! Quite a lot! Well, at least she has got upset. I suppose I can't know for sure what the other parents thought. **Can you imagine that anything else could happen?** Some days she goes in a bit better. If I claimed her a reward for going in without a fuss that might help her feel more positively about going in. **Have you ever seen that happen to someone else?** When Jenny first started in this class a few of the children were super going in. **What would you think was happening if someone else was in the same boat?** I wouldn't think anything about the parents at all apart from poor them. **Can you imagine that anything else could happen?** Well I suppose other parents might think the same. Especially if they can see I am doing my best to help Jenny.	**What did you think?** I thought, I can offer her a reward to help her feel better about going in to school, but even if she does get upset, the other parents won't necessarily think badly of me. They might even be sympathetic. **What did you do?** Talked to Jenny about her fears about going in to school and worked through one of these charts with her. She seemed to feel a bit better about it after that, but to encourage her more I said we could stop for a cake on the way home if she went in without a fuss. **How did you feel?** I felt much better for having a plan for what I'd do with Jenny. As I approached school I felt more confident that we could both handle it, which meant I could relax and focus on my plan.

TABLE 12.3: HELPING MYSELF WITH UNHELPFUL THOUGHTS: PARENTS' WORRIES ABOUT SARAH

What is happening?	What am I thinking?	Evidence and alternatives	What happened in the end?
There is a spider in the corner of the room and Sarah is about to catch sight of it.	**Why are you worried?** She is going to freak out when she sees that spider. **What do you think will happen?** She will get really upset and we won't be able to calm her down – it will put a downer on the whole day.	**What makes you think that this will happen?** She has freaked out in the past and it has been really difficult. **Can you imagine that anything else could happen?** Well, in theory she might not freak out. Occasionally it hasn't been so bad. And recently we have found helped her not get so upset. **If it did happen, could there be any other reasons for it?** It had it seems worse when she is tired or hungry. She is neither of those things now, so it may not be too bad. Also we have different ways of handling it now so even if she does get upset it needn't spoil the whole day. **What would you think was happening if someone else was in the same boat?** She's only going to get over the fear by facing it – maybe this is a good opportunity for us to help her look at the spider from a distance.	**What did you think?** We thought "She might get really upset, but then again she might not." Let's take this opportunity to help her face her fear. **What did you do?** We made out we were really pleased and excited because we now had a chance to do the next step on her chart and for her to get her reward. We told her hand and all looked at the spider from a distance. She was nervous but afterwards she didn't lose control! Afterwards she had her reward. **How did you feel?** We felt a bit nervous initially but then relaxed. Sarah felt really pleased with herself.

Do as I do

Your child won't just be picking up on how you react when *he or she* faces a fear. He or she will also be picking up on how *you* react to the scary thing yourself. If a child sees a parent dealing with fears by trying to avoid them, rather than facing up to them, then it is likely that the child will learn to do the same. On the other hand, if a parent can show a child that he or she is able to face fears and overcome them then this will serve as encouragement to the child. You need to face your own fears in order to help your child face his or her own. This, of course, is not always easy; but it is fine for your child to see that you, too, are experiencing difficulty, as he or she will also undoubtedly struggle at times to overcome fears. The tips that we have provided in Chapter 9 may be useful for you in facing your fears, in particular taking a gradual, step-by-step approach.

Getting your child involved

Again, your child may be able to help you draw up your own step-by-step plan and may even be able to reward you for your achievements. Getting your child involved in this way can be good for a number of reasons: (i) it shows your child the strategies you are using to overcome your fear; (ii) it puts your child in a position of control and being the 'expert'; (iii) having someone to push you along will help your motivation; and (iv) it will make it all more fun! Remember to refer back to the first four steps for tips on generating helpful thoughts, rewards and step-by-step plans.

Here's an example of the step-by-step plan that Jenny and her mum came up with to overcome Mum's fear of cats.

BOX 12.3 MUM'S STEP-BY-STEP PLAN

Ultimate goal: let the cat sit on my lap (and stroke it) for at least 5 minutes.

Helpful thought:

Ultimate reward: night out with friends (Jenny with sitter).

Step 8: let neighbour put the cat on my lap.

Helpful thought:

Reward: trip to cinema with Jenny.

Step 7: stroke the cat while it sits on the neighbour's lap.

Helpful thought:

Reward: breakfast in bed made by Jenny.

Step 6: sit next to neighbour with the cat on her lap.

Helpful thought:

Reward: make a cake with Jenny.

Step 5: talk to neighbour in her living room with the cat in the room.

Helpful thought:

Reward: peaceful bubble bath with no interruptions.

Step 4: talk to neighbour with neighbour holding the cat.

Helpful thought:

Reward: Jenny will help with some housework.

Step 3: talk to neighbour (who has a cat) just inside their front door.

Helpful thought:

Reward: a cup of tea made by Jenny.

Step 2: talk to neighbour (who has a cat) at their front door (where the cat could run out).

Helpful thought:

Reward: praise from Jenny.

Step 1: look at pictures of cats in a book.

Helpful thought: these cats can't hurt me. I'll be fine.

Reward: praise from Jenny.

Creating the right opportunities

From the examples in the step-by-step plans in this book, it is clear that we can't always just wait for the right situation to arise for a child to be able to face a fear. If we want him or her to face it, and in a gradual manner, we need to create the opportunities for this to happen. This may mean liaising with a teacher (as we saw in Jenny's step-by-step plan, Step 5) or other people who may be able to help, or collect materials (like dead and alive spiders, as we did in Sarah's step-by-step plan).

As we know, Jenny's mum also felt anxious in social situations, in particular those where she felt others were judging her. Approaching Jenny's teacher was, therefore, quite a difficult thing for her to do. Similarly, we also know Sarah's parents weren't that keen on spiders, so the job of collecting spiders was not something that they relished. Here is another area, then, where it is important to be aware of whether your own anxiety could get in the way of what you are trying to do to help your child move forward. If it is, then maybe the task you need to do to help your child could form the ultimate goal for your own step-by-step plan?

Encouraging problem solving

If your child is seeing you spending a lot of time worrying, then it is likely that he or she is not seeing you finding constructive ways to solve problems. People who worry a lot often feel that by worrying they are 'doing something' about their problems, but this is not true: as we discussed in the last chapter, worry rarely solves problems. We don't know why some people believe that worry is a good way to deal with problems, but it is likely that it is because this is how they have seen others around them deal with problems and they are not experienced with other ways of sorting problems out. We are sure that you can see where this is going. You need to use problem solving, too. By doing this you will be helping yourself, and also showing your child a constructive way to deal with problems, which will encourage him or her to do the same.

If this isn't enough

Reading through this chapter you may have recognized your own thoughts and behaviors and you may have now tried out the strategies discussed for yourself. You may feel, however, that the fears or worries that you are faced with are too great to tackle on your own. In this case you may find it helpful to seek professional support in overcoming these difficulties. Your general practitioner can advise you on how to obtain this sort of support locally. At the end of this book you will also find a Useful Resources section which includes reading materials as well as information on organizations aimed at adults experiencing emotional difficulties. It is our experience that where parents are able to overcome their own fears and worries this helps them enormously with helping their child overcome his or her own.

MANAGING YOUR OWN ANXIETY: KEY POINTS

• If a parent is very anxious this can make it more difficult for him or her to help a child to overcome anxiety.

• Let your child know that everyone experiences some fears and worries sometimes.

• Demonstrate to your child how you deal positively with fears and worries using helpful thinking, step-by-step plans and problem solving.

• If fear is stopping you from creating opportunities for your child to face fears, then set conquering this fear as your own ultimate goal.

• If further help is needed, do not be afraid to ask for it. It could benefit both you and your child.

13

Some final words on the guide: Keeping it going

We hope that you are now feeling more and more confident about applying the strategies we have discussed in the previous chapters. Now it is just a case of keeping going! As you can see from the gradual approach that we take to facing fears, the problems experienced with fears and worries are unlikely to go away overnight. It takes perseverance to keep working towards your child's ultimate goals. In our clinic we typically work with parents for a period of about two months. In that time we would expect there to be noticeable changes, but we would not necessarily expect ultimate goals to have been reached. If they have, then there are often new goals to strive for. It is rarely the end of the work. Within that period of time, however, we find that families have normally had a good chance to put their new skills into practise and we often feel confident that they no longer need our help and can continue working on their goals as a family. From then on we encourage families to keep practising the skills that they have learned, as this is the best way to keep progress going.

When progress is slow

At times it may feel as if you are not making progress, so at these times it is important to return to your early notes and compare how things are now with how things were when you started trying to help your child overcome their anxieties. You may be pleasantly surprised by the progress that has been made. However, if progress is slow, you will need to make sure you have clear goals to focus on. In addition, it is likely that some skills we have described worked particularly well with your child, whereas your child may have taken to others less well. It will be useful to remember which things particularly seemed to help your child for those times in the future when you want to make a concerted effort to help him or her face a particular fear.

What has helped your child?

On the following page, make a note of the things that you have found particularly helped your child to overcome anxiety, so that you can refer back to this in the future.

Problems you may face

The table 13.1 describes some specific problems that parents have told us they found as they tried to overcome their child's fears and worries. We urge you not to be put off by these problems, but to use the skills that you and your child have been practising with this book to overcome them. So, rather than telling you what to do we have made some suggestions for strategies you might be able to use to find your own solution (just as we have been encouraging you to do when helping your child). This way you are putting into practice the skills you have learned and also coming up with solutions that are going to suit you.

BOX 13.1 THINGS I HAVE DONE THAT HAVE BEEN
HELPFUL FOR REDUCING MY CHILD'S ANXIETY

One common problem that arises is when two parents have different approaches to the management of their child's anxious feelings and behaviors. This was the case for Jenny's parents. They had separated a few years earlier but tried to get along with each other for Jenny's sake, but they both found it difficult. One thing they disagreed about was Jenny's anxiety. Jenny's dad felt that her mum mollycoddled her and that Jenny should just be told to get on with it. Her mum, however, felt that the dad was too strict and did not show Jenny enough understanding. The problem was made worse by the fact that the more Jenny's mum tried to be sympathetic and supportive the more the dad thought she was being mollycoddled – making him more strict and firm with Jenny. And the more he was strict and firm, the more Jenny's mum wanted to protect her. As the main carer, Jenny's mum embarked on this program to overcome Jenny's anxiety, but the program stopped when Jenny went to visit her dad. Jenny's mum was concerned that she and her ex-husband have such different ideas about how to manage Jenny's anxiety that they were not being consistent, and that because there were gaps of a week at a time when nothing was happening towards overcoming Jenny's anxiety, they were making slow progress. Jenny's mum sat down with a problem-solving chart to try to work out a solution to this problem. What she came up with is shown in Table 13.2.

Keep it going

If things have been going well and your child has made great progress, then it will be tempting to stop practising the techniques and sit back and reap the rewards of your hard work! You must, however, keep on your toes and be on the lookout for opportunities to continue using the strategies. The more familiar your child is with the strategies, the more they will become your child's habitual way of dealing with problems and the better prepared he or she will be for dealing with any problems that she or he faces throughout life and for avoiding becoming highly anxious in the future.

When Sarah was able to hold a spider in her hand she and her parents had got further than they had imagined. That did not stop them continuing to use their new skills, however. Whenever any situation came up in the future that worried Sarah they continued to help her think 'helpful thoughts', encouraged her to face her fears (rather than avoid them) or problem solve to find a solution. They noticed that with time Sarah seemed automatically to consider different explanations for her worries. Where there was a genuine problem, rather than letting it cause her a great deal of worry, she focused on what she needed to do to sort out the problem. As her life progressed she became a resourceful and resilient young woman.

TABLE 13.1: COMMON PROBLEMS THAT PARENTS FACE IN OVERCOMING THEIR CHILD'S FEARS, WORRIES AND ANXIETY

Problem	Tips for finding a solution
1. Practical problems (i) I don't have enough time to do the exercises.	Try 'problem solving'.
(ii) It's quicker (easier) to just do something for my child, rather than try to get him or her to do it him-or herself.	Is this really true when you think about it in the long term as well as the short term?

Problem	Tips for finding a solution
(iii) I don't know when to push my child. Is he or she anxious or is he or she not interested?	Is there a strategy that you could use whatever the reason (such as rewards)?
(iv) Other family members have different ideas about what is the right thing to do.	Try 'problem solving'. Could you share other chapters in this book with your family?
(v) When my child 'acts up' I don't know if this is because he orshe upset orbeing difficult.	Again, is there a strategy that you could use whatever the reason (such as rewards)? Also see Chapter 17 on overcoming difficult behavior.
(vi) I'm not there at the times that my child worries about.	Try 'problem solving'.
(vii) It seems unfair to my other children to be rewarding one child for doing things that they do all the time.	Try 'problem solving'. Is there anything your other children would benefit from being rewarded for?
(viii) We know what our child needs to do to overcome his or her fears, but those situations just don't happen very often in everyday life.	Try 'problem solving'. Also think about creating the right opportunities.
2. Personal problems	
(i) I find it hard to keep motivated to keep 'pushing' my child.	See Chapter 12 on managing your own anxiety. Try 'problem solving'.
(ii) I can't help worrying about how my child will be able to manage if I give them a push.	What is it that worries you? Could there be another way of thinking about this?
(iii) It's hard to push my child to do something, when other members of the family have the same problem and aren't doing anything about it.	Try 'problem solving'.

TABLE 13.2: JENNY'S MUM'S PROBLEM SOLVING

What is the problem?	List all the possible solutions	What would happen if I chose this solution? (In the short term? In the long term? To my anxiety in the future?)	Is this plan doable? Yes/No	How good is this plan? Rate 0–10	What happened?
Jenny's dad and I treat Jenny's anxiety differently so the program is not getting followed consistently.	1. Carry on as I am.	1. Nothing would change. I'd carry on trying and may make some progress, but it would be much slower than if we were both on board.	Yes	5	
	2. Talk to Jenny's dad about what I've been doing and ask him to do the same.	2. He would think I was criticizing him. We'd get into an argument. Unlikely much would change.	Yes	1	
	3. Give Jenny's dad what I have been reading and show him my records of what I've done so far.	3. He could take it away and read it, then he is less likely to feel criticized. If he sees the progress she has made so far he may think it's worth a try. If he doesn't there's nothing to lose.	Yes	8	Gave Jenny's dad the book with my notes in it. He didn't seem to like the look of it but took it anyway. Has just called and said he'll give it a go.

Future goals

Have a think now about what you feel it is important for you and your child to continue to work on. Make a note of this in the box below so that you can refer back to this in the future to see whether you have begun to work towards those goals and what progress you have made.

BOX 13.2 THINGS FOR ME AND MY CHILD TO CONTINUE TO WORK ON

1 _____

2 _____

3 _____

4 _____

5 _____

6 _____

7 _____

8 _____

9 _____

10 _____

Tom met his ultimate goal of sleeping in his bedroom on his own, but once he had achieved that it became clear to his parents that, because of his fears about separation, there were still certain things he would not do. For example, Tom had been invited to a sleepover party but had insisted that his parents pick him up before everyone went to sleep. Tom's parents also longed for a night out together yet had never been able to get a babysitter for Tom as he found the idea terrifying. Tom's parents generated the following list of goals to continue to work on.

> ## BOX 13.3 THINGS FOR US TO CONTINUE TO WORK ON WITH TOM
>
> 1 Tom to stay at home with a babysitter.
>
> 2 Tom to go on day trip with school without parents.
>
> 3 Tom to stay away from home overnight (with a friend/grandparents).
>
> 4 Tom to go to scout camp.

Reward yourself!

Finally, we would like you to take this opportunity to stop and think about the achievements that you and your child have made. Throughout the program you will have been rewarding your child for his or her efforts and we hope that you will continue to do so. At this point though, you should also acknowledge that if your child has made progress then it has been down to the help that you have been giving him or her. Although we are sure that your child's progress is a reward in itself, perhaps the time has come to reward yourself for all the work that you have put in to make this happen. Have a nice meal or a long bath, arrange a night out, get together with a friend. Whatever you do, just be sure to mark the occasion and give yourself the credit that you deserve for helping your child overcome his or her fears and worries.

Ben's parents really struggled to help Ben overcome his fear of 'Drog'. One of the things that they found most difficult, but most helpful, was taking the time to talk to Ben about Drog and taking his concerns seriously. It was surprisingly hard to not just say, 'Don't be silly, Ben. There is no Drog!' They persevered, however, and made an effort to take their time and help Ben work out for himself that Drog was not a real danger to him. Their efforts paid off, and within a month Ben had reached the top of his step-by-step plan and was able to play happily upstairs, even when no one else was within hearing distance. To reward him for all his hard work, Ben received his ultimate reward of a trip to a theme park. Ben's parents could see the hard work that Ben had put in, but they also had to acknowledge that nothing would have changed if they had not worked so hard to give Ben the support and encouragement he needed. So they asked a relative to come round, and Ben's parents treated themselves to a well-deserved night out!

KEEP IT GOING: KEY POINTS

- Keep practising the skills you have learned.
- Keep working towards new goals.
- Use these skills to overcome problems along the way.

- Reward yourself for the work that you have done and the progress you have made. Well done!

PART THREE

Addressing Particular Needs

14

Using this book with younger children

Throughout this book, we have mostly talked about helping children of all ages overcome anxiety. However, you will have noticed from our examples that we have tended to focus on children from primary school age to early teens. If your child is about eight years of age or younger we suggest that you read this chapter after you have read through Part Two, but before you actually start to embark on the program. This will give you some tips on ways to make the most of the program with a younger child.

How much anxiety is normal in younger children?

It is common for young children to get anxious about all kinds of things. It is part of growing up and learning about the world. For example, toddlers are often startled by loud noises whereas four- and five-year-olds are often afraid of monsters or the dark. This is normal and it is likely that your child will simply grow out of these fears. The strategies in this chapter will, however, be useful to prevent these fears becoming a problem. This chapter will also be helpful to address any fears that may have been appropriate for your child's age in the past but which have persisted while other children have grown out of them. It will also, of course, be useful for any case in which a fear or worry is getting in your child's way (for example, stopping him or her doing things that he or she would enjoy doing).

What do I need to do differently with younger children?

In Part Two we have described a whole range of strategies that you can use to help your child overcome anxiety. We will now discuss which of these strategies work best with younger children and talk about ways in which you can adapt these ideas to help a young child to use them.

Changing anxious thoughts

We talked in Chapter 4 about helping your child to change anxious thoughts. Younger children are likely to find the process of spotting thoughts, examining evidence and coming up with alternative ways of thinking far too complicated. What is essential for young children to learn, however, is that there can be different ways of thinking about the same situation and that we sometimes need to put our ideas to the test to find out if they are correct. So, the principle is the same as we discussed in Part Two; however, you will need to be taking a more active role in helping your child become aware of other ways of thinking and how he or she could test out different ideas. This involves three basic steps: (i) finding out what your child is frightened of; (ii) coming up with other ways of thinking about the situation; and (iii) putting different ways of thinking to the test.

STEP 1: WHAT IS FRIGHTENING YOUR CHILD?

The first step is, of course, finding out exactly what your child is afraid of in the situation. Ask simple questions, using simple language, such as 'What do you think is going to happen?' Young children often find it easier to describe something happening to someone else rather than themselves so, for example, use dolls or action figures to set up a story about a situation that would frighten your child, and see what happens to the dolls in the story that your child creates. Your child may tell quite a fantastical story but you are likely to be able to pick up themes from the story. For example, does he or she think he or she will get hurt, or that someone else will get hurt? Or that someone will get lost or taken away?

STEP 2: OTHER WAYS OF THINKING

The next step is to help your child consider that other things could happen apart from the feared outcome.

Give your child suggestions of other ways to think about a frightening situation that will help him or her to create a positive image of him- or herself coping with the situation. Using dolls as we described above, bring in a new character and show how the character would cope in the feared situation. You can also think about your child's favourite characters from television or books, and create a story in which this character overcomes the same fear. Importantly, this doesn't mean simply showing the character in the situation not feeling scared. Your child will relate to the story more if, just like your child, the character feels scared but doesn't let it stop him or her from having a good time. Use pictures and toys to illustrate this or build it into a bedtime story. This can then be used as a reminder when your child enters a similar situation – for example, 'Remember what Bob the Builder did?', 'OK, Dora the Explorer, what are you going to do now?'

An example of a bedtime story that Joe's mum told Joe is below.

Mum: 'Postman Pat was delivering his letters when he got to a house and heard a dog barking. It sounded like a really big dog. How do you think Postman Pat felt?'

Joe: 'Scared.'

Mum: 'Yes, Postman Pat felt quite scared when he heard the dog. But Postman Pat had a letter to deliver and nothing was going to stop him. So what do you think he did?'

Joe: 'I don't know.'

Mum: 'Well, first he wanted to know how big the dog was so he went up to the window and had a look in. When he looked in the window, guess who he saw?'

Joe: 'The dog.'

Mum: 'Yes, he did see the dog, and it was quite a big dog, but he also saw Sam Hedges. It was Sam's house. Sam saw Pat looking through the window. "Hello, Pat," he called, "Oh, I see you've seen Tessie. She's my brother's dog and she's staying with me this week while he's on holiday. She makes a lot of noise but she's very friendly. Why don't you come in for a cup of tea?" Sam let Pat in and Tessie came up and licked his hands. She was very friendly. Then Sam made Pat a lovely cup of tea before Pat got on with his rounds.'

STEP 3: PUTTING IDEAS TO THE TEST

In Part Two we encouraged you to help your child to work out how to test out fears for him- or herself. With younger children you will need to be more active in giving ideas of how to test frightening thoughts. Here's an example.

Joe: 'I don't like Granddad's dog.'

Mum: 'Why don't you like the dog?'

Joe: 'It might bite me.'

> Mum: 'Has the dog ever bitten Granddad?'
>
> Joe: 'I don't know.'
>
> Mum: 'Let's ask Granddad and find out.'

Changing anxious behavior

GIVING ATTENTION TO ' HAVE A GO' BEHAVIOR

In Chapter 8 we talked about how you can encourage your child to 'have a go' at things that make him or her anxious. We talked about making sure you give your child lots of attention and praise when he or she is being brave, and trying not to give too much attention when he or she is anxious. Young children are especially sensitive to the messages they receive from their parents, so this principle is particularly important. We know that if we praise or give attention to good behavior (such as eating nicely at dinner), your child is more likely to do this again, whereas if we ignore bad behavior (such as a tantrum) this behavior is less likely to happen again.

Children start to learn at an early age that their actions have consequences. At less than two years of age children recognize praise and will behave in a way that is likely to attract it. Immediate rewards (such as stickers) will also act to reinforce positive behavior from about three years of age, and from four years or so children will be able to alter their behavior with the promise of slightly less immediate rewards (for example, using star charts to save up for a reward). So we need to be paying attention to children's positive and 'have a go' behavior from an early age and responding to it with clear praise.

Your child is now learning that when she or he 'has a go' and faces fears good things happen. It is also important that he or she learns that when he or she is not able to face fears *nothing bad happens,* but, at the same time, *nothing good happens.* When your child refuses to 'have a go' or becomes anxious or distressed it would be wrong to ignore your child completely, but what you can do is ignore the *fear* and the *anxious behavior.* The simplest way to do this is to distract your child to help get his or her mind off the fear, but without removing him or her from the situation (and encouraging avoidance). So, for example, if your child becomes nervous as he or she approaches the school playground, change the conversation to point out something happening in the distance ('Wow, look at that cat'), talk about something good that will be happening today, or what he or she would like to do after school. By using this strategy you are not giving attention to your child's fear and he or she is helped to cope with the fear. He or she also starts to discover that just because something seems scary at first it doesn't mean he or she can't deal with it, and he or she may even end up enjoying it!

USING A STEP-BY-STEP PLAN WITH A YOUNGER CHILD

Just as with older children, a step-by-step plan is a useful way to help your child gradually build up the number of things he or she can 'have a go' at.

Once again, where we previously encouraged you to help your child to devise the step-by-step plan him- or herself, with younger children you will have to take a more active role and create the step-by-step plan for your child. As before, identify an ultimate goal and work out a series of gradual steps to build up to this goal. State clear rewards that you know will motivate your child to have a go at each step. If your child is reluctant to have a go then the step is too big and will need breaking down. An example of Joe's step-by-step plan is on the facing page.

Encouraging your child to become independent

Lots of parents of young children talk about how hard it is to 'let go'. By this they mean letting their child become more independent, by going to nursery or school, leaving them with friends or relatives or encouraging them to do things by themselves. It can be particularly difficult to do these things if your child is very anxious. We talked about the importance of encouraging your child to develop independence in Chapter 8, Step 3. Anxious children often expect that they won't be able to cope in difficult situations and feel that they need to be protected by their parents. In turn, their parents protect them because they know how upsetting these situations might be. This means a vicious cycle develops, in which your child never gets to learn that he or she can cope (and how to cope). By using the step-by-step plan not only will your child gradually face the fear, but you will also gradually get used to letting him or her have a go and becoming more independent.

Everyday life

The strategies described in this chapter will help your child to recognize that there are different ways of thinking about situations, encouraging him or her to put different explanations to the test, and then to 'have a go' and not let fear get in the way. These can be thought of as good skills for life.

BOX 14.1 JOE'S STEP-BY-STEP PLAN

Ultimate goal: to stroke the dog when Granddad is not holding her.

Helpful thought:

Ultimate reward: a day trip to the beach.

Step 7: stroke the dog on her head while Granddad holds her.

Helpful thought:

Reward: choose a DVD on the way home.

Step 6: to touch the dog while Granddad holds her.

Helpful thought:

Reward: have a friend round for tea.

Step 5: to stay in the living room while Granddad takes the dog off the lead and holds her.

Helpful thought:

Reward: buy a sweet on the way home.

Step 4: to go for a walk round the block with Granddad, taking the dog on the lead.

Helpful thought:

Reward: buy a comic on the way home.

Step 3: to stay in the living room when Granddad brings the dog in on a lead.

Helpful thought:

Reward: go to the park on the way home.

Step 2: to go into Granddad's living room when the dog is in the kitchen.

Helpful thought:

Reward: play with Granddad's toy cars.

Step 1: to go in to Granddad's house when the dog is in the garden.

Helpful thought: I'm Postman Pat and nothing's going to stop me delivering my letter to Granddad!

Reward: a sweet from Granddad's tin.

BOX 14.2 TIPS FOR SUCCESSFUL REWARDS WITH YOUNGER CHILDREN

• Make sure your child understands what he or she will get as a reward if he or she can 'have a go' at a step on the plan ('if you come into the living room with Tessie, we'll go to the park on the way home').

• Be clear what he or she is getting the reward for ('Well done, because you managed to say hello to the lady at the checkout, we'll go and make the cakes now').

• Reward your child every time he or she does each step, not just once.

• Give your child the reward immediately after he or she has completed the step, or as soon as possible afterwards (if necessary buy the reward beforehand so you have it ready to give to your child).

• Often with younger children, rewards that involve *doing* things with you are more effective than material rewards (that is, buying things).

• Give your child lots of praise as well for completing the step ('Well done for having your friend round, you were really brave and Daddy is very proud of you').

Take opportunities to encourage your child to learn these principles during everyday life and make them a part of your lifestyle. They will stand your child in good stead for dealing with problems that he or she will encounter long into the future.

USING THIS BOOK WITH YOUNGER CHILDREN: KEY POINTS

• Help your child to describe what he or she fears, using dolls or stories.

• Suggest other ways of thinking and ways of testing out different ideas.

• Encourage 'have a go' behavior with praise and rewards.

• Distract your child from fears and worries.

• Use a step-by-step plan to face fears gradually.

• Take opportunities to practise these strategies in everyday life.

15

Using this book with teenagers

Throughout most of this book, we have talked about helping children of all ages overcome fears and worries. However, you will have noticed from our examples that we have tended to focus on children from primary school age to early teens. This chapter focuses on helping older children overcome their anxiety using some of the strategies we have already talked about, such as changing anxious thoughts.

How can I help my teenager overcome anxiety?

Helping your teenager to overcome his or her anxiety will not be easy. Teenagers are often more likely to be reluctant to cooperate and may think that you are simply interfering. They are also likely to be particularly sensitive to what they think other people are thinking about them. One of the biggest challenges you will face is talking to your teenager in a way that lets him or her feel that you are genuinely interested in his or her point of view and take this seriously. If you can successfully show your adolescent that you understand his or her anxiety problems, then you are well on your way to helping overcome them. As we discussed at the beginning of Part Two it is not just *what* you say and do that will be important, but also *how* you say or do it. For your teenager to work with you, you need to show that you understand and accept what he or she is worried about. You are not criticizing or judging him or her; however, you do recognize that this worry is getting in the way and something needs to be done about it.

Does your teenager want to change?

Although you may view your teenager's worries as being problematic, it is possible that he or she does not feel the same way. For your teenager to make progress he or she will need to want to make changes. If he or she does not then we would suggest not trying to embark upon this program at the moment. You will need to wait until your teenager is ready to work with you. Telling your child that he or she *has* to do the things in this book will lead to more reluctance on his or her part. Instead, listen to your teenager and show that you understand his or her point of view. Ask about his or her goals and whether fears or worries will create any difficulties in achieving them. In the end, the choice is your child's, but your job is to help him or her make an *informed* choice.

An example of a conversation between Jill, a teenager who was scared of the dark, and her father is overleaf.

What do I need to do differently with my teenager?

If your teenager has made the choice to have a go at overcoming his or her fears or worries you are over halfway there. All the strategies that we have discussed in Part Two work well with adolescents. We will now highlight some points to consider when using these strategies with an older child or teenager.

Father: 'Jill, I've bought this book about helping young people to overcome their fears because I thought it might help you with your fear of the dark. From reading it I can see I would need you to be working with me for it to work, how do you feel about that?'

Jill: 'I don't need to work on anything. I'm fine how I am.'

Father: 'Well, if you are fine how you are then that's OK. I suppose it doesn't necessarily get in your way that much, does it?'

Jill: 'No. I just keep the light on when I go to sleep.'

Father: 'Yes, and that's not a problem at home. Is there anywhere that that would create a problem?'

Jill: 'Not really. I guess if I went to stay at other people's houses it might, if they didn't want the light on when they went to sleep.'

Father: 'Yes, but you don't really go and stay at other people's houses. Is that something you'd like to do if you weren't scared of the dark?'

Jill: 'Maybe.'

Father: 'I've never really asked you this before, but what do you imagine your life being like in ten years' time?'

Jill: 'I don't know. I hope I'd have a good job. Maybe I'd be married and have children by then.'

Father: 'Do you think your fear of the dark could get in the way of you getting to that point at all?'

Jill: 'I don't think so ... maybe, if I met someone who couldn't sleep with the light on.'

Father: 'So it sounds like your fear of the dark isn't a huge problem right now, but you might be happier going to sleepovers if it was sorted out. Right now you might have a problem if you were staying with someone who didn't like having the light on. I guess we've got two options: to stay the same or to try to overcome the fear. It really is up to you, but as long as you know I'd like to help if you decide if you want to go for it. OK?'

Giving adolescents more control

The main difference in helping adolescents overcome their anxiety is that they need to be put in a position of greater control over the strategies that they use. Although they still need your support and guidance, they will be much more capable of carrying out some of the strategies independently, and, in fact, they are likely to want to do them independently, rather than have you tell them what to do! It is really important to remember this. If you insist on taking charge, your teenager is likely to lose interest and refuse to participate at all. You may also want to encourage them to get their friends involved, or other adults that they know well. Although parents want to help, sometimes your teenager will welcome help from others more than from you. A good starting point might be to get your teenager to read this book to decide whether he or she thinks it is worth a try. Immediately, you are giving him or her more control, rather than telling him or her what to do. Then, perhaps you can ask him or her which strategy he or she wants to work on first, which one makes most sense and how he or she would like you to help. In this way, you are allowing your teenager to take the lead. It is also worth asking who else he or she thinks might be able to help him or her have a go at some of the tasks in this book. Are there friends or other adults who could provide a bit of support?

Changing anxious thoughts

In Chapters 6 and 7 we talked about how anxious children experience anxious or unhelpful thoughts and how changing these thoughts and coming up with more helpful thoughts can reduce anxiety. These strategies work particularly well with adolescents who have the ability to notice their anxious thoughts and try to change them. In those chapters we talked about how you, as a parent, could try to find out what your child's anxious or unhelpful thoughts are and then help your child to test the evidence for his or her own thoughts. With adolescents, you can use the same process. However, your adolescent may well get the hang of this quite quickly, in which case he or she can then start to write down and challenge his or her own thoughts without your help. You don't want your teenager to feel as if he or she is now going it alone, however, so review the record sheet with him or her every few days or even once a week, and congratulate him or her on how well he or she is challenging unhelpful thoughts.

Praise and rewards

Chapter 8 was about encouraging your child to 'have a go' and face fears. Although the concept of rewards may seem quite childish it can still be a powerful motivator with older children and adolescents. Its success depends on the choice of rewards. Of course, you must agree to the rewards before your teenager starts to face his or her fears, so that he or she does not do so thinking that he or she will achieve something unrealistic, but it must be your teenager who makes the choice, as only he or she will know what will motivate him or her to face his or her fears. In contrast to younger children, doing things with you is likely to be less of a motivator – but coming up with ways that you can facilitate activities that he or she can do with friends will provide good alternatives to material and financial rewards.

Using a step-by-step plan with an adolescent

Chapter 9 described how to make a step-by-step plan to help your child enter into situations that may make him or her anxious. A step-by-step plan is a useful tool for children of any age, and indeed adults too! With an adolescent, you do not necessarily need to call it a step-by-step plan, you can refer to it as a ladder or hierarchy, but the principle remains the same. Your adolescent needs to stop avoiding situations that make him or her anxious. He or she needs to 'have a go' gradually at doing things that make him or her anxious, starting with the easiest and moving up to the hardest as he or she grows more confident and becomes less anxious. The step-by-step plan gives a clear plan of action with lots of small goals leading to the ultimate goal. Without a clear plan, it is more likely that your teenager will continue to avoid those situations that make him or her anxious.

Problem-solving skills

In Chapter 10 we talked about how you can help your child to solve problems. The problem-solving strategies we discussed are particularly useful for adolescents. Adolescence is a time when your child should be becoming more independent, and one part of this process is for him or her to be able to start dealing with tricky situations on his or her own. The problem-solving steps we described in Step 5 are a good way of starting to do just this.

Initially, as with challenging unhelpful thoughts, you will need to teach your child how to problem solve, by working through the steps together. However, once he or she has got the hang of these, he or she can start to do it more independently. Your child should be able to come up with a list of possible solutions and to be able to rate them in terms of how good they are and how doable they are. He or she may want to check with you whether his or her preferred solution is a good one, and it is important that you remember to ask how he or she got on with putting the chosen solution into action.

USING THIS BOOK WITH TEENAGERS: KEY POINTS

• Show your teenager genuine interest in his or her thoughts. Maintain a non-judgmental manner.

• Help your teenager make an informed choice about whether to try to overcome his or her fears or worries.

• Follow the steps described in Part Two, but allow your teenager to be in control as much as possible.

16

Sleep problems

Problems at night-time are extremely common among anxious children. Many children whom we work with find it very difficult to drop off to sleep. Sometimes it is particularly difficult for children if there is nobody with them, so your child may like you to stay with him or her as he or she goes to sleep, or he or she may sleep in your bed with you. Your child may also wake frequently during the night and find it very hard to get back to sleep and feel the need to come and seek you out during the night.

This is all exhausting for parents. It can mean that you are getting very little time to yourself or for you and your partner to be together, and it can mean you are functioning on minimal (and broken) sleep. As all parents know from having young babies, this can be very draining. When you are tired it is extremely difficult to be the patient person that you might otherwise be, and you are likely to, at times, feel resentful of this time that your child is demanding when you just need some time to yourself.

At other times parents may simply feel resigned to the fact that this is just how things are going to be. If it is not causing anyone a problem now then that may be absolutely fine. If, for example, you are all getting enough sleep, it is not affecting relationships within the family and it is not stopping your child doing things that other children his or her age are doing (such as going to sleepovers and having friends to stay). You do need to think carefully, however, about how much longer the current situation will be acceptable. Will you still be happy about things being the same when your child is eight? Ten? Starting secondary school? Starting work? The point we are making is that if your child is having night-time difficulties this situation should not be accepted as permanent. Change can be made.

Is good sleep being promoted?

First and foremost you need to be certain that the environment is right for your child to be able to go to sleep. Run through the simple checklist on the facing page.

Night-time fears

Having established an environment that is going to help (not hinder) your child's sleep, the focus now turns to your child. The main reasons for sleep problems in anxious children are:

1 Fear of being alone or separated from a loved one.

2 Fear of the dark.

3 Uncontrollable worry (not necessarily about a
   specific fear).

In order to know exactly how best to approach your
child's night-time fears and worries you need to know,
of course, exactly what it is that your child is
concerned about. There may be simple practical steps
that you can adopt that will become clear once you
have a good understanding of your child's fear. For
example, if your child is worried that he or she will
need to go to the toilet in the night but will trip in
the dark, then you could put a plug-in night-light on
the landing.

TABLE 16.1: SLEEP CHECKLIST

	If yes:
1. Is your child's bedroom too hot?	Turn the heaters down. Open windows slightly. Use a fan.
2. Is your child's bedroom too cold?	Turn the heaters up. Add a blanket.
3. Is your child's bed uncomfortable?	Change the mattress/bed. Change the bedding.
4. Is your child's room too light?	Hang a towel over the curtain or invest in blackout blinds.
5. Is your child's room too dark?	Use a night-light.
6. Is your child's room too noisy?	The solution depends on the source of the noise. Can you ask people to be quieter? Can the room be insulated at all (such as hanging a heavy towel over the window)?
7. Are there distractions keeping your child awake (such as television, DVD, computer games)?	Restrict their use or remove them!

	If yes:
8. Is your child tired enough?	Cut down/cut out daytime naps if your child has them. Wake your child earlier. Build an outdoor activity into your early-evening routine (but not too near to bedtime, so there is plenty of time to wind down).
9. Is your child 'charged up' at bedtime (from playing computer games, watching DVDs, for example)?	Restrict these exciting activities to earlier times in the day.
10. Is your child drinking a lot before bed?	Cut down/cut out drinks in the hour before bedtime. Make sure your child visits the toilet before bed.
11. Is your child eating/drinking caffeine before bed?	Cut down/cut out caffeinated drinks/foods (such as cola, chocolate) in the hours before bedtime.
12. Does your child's body not know when to go to bed?	Make sure your child has a regular bedtime routine (do the same things in the same order before bed) and goes to bed at the same time each day.

The strategies described in Part Two are all suitable for dealing with bedtime worries. As with other fears we would recommend you follow the five steps:

1 Work out what your child fears about going to bed.

2 Help your child to consider other ways of thinking about this fear.

3 Encourage and praise your child's attempts to overcome this fear.

4 Set up a step-by-step plan which builds up to your child sleeping in his or her own bed alone all night.

5 Work with your child to help him or her solve any problems that occur.

A step-by-step approach to helping your child sleep alone

As we have discussed earlier, something that is common to anxious people (children and adults) is the view that the world is a dangerous place and that they have no control over this. Throughout this book our emphasis has been on finding ways to help your child discover that the world is not always or necessarily so frightening, and that, in fact, he or she has the power to make a difference to what happens. When it comes to night-time, we want to give your child the opportunity to learn that, for example, he or she can be alone and can cope. By adopting a step-by-step approach your child will not be put straight into a terrifying situation, but will instead gradually build up what he or she is able to do. In order to draw up a step-by-step plan with your child, read through Chapter 9 again carefully. A fairly typical example of this in relation to fear of sleeping alone is shown on the facing page in Tom's step-by-step plan.

BOX 16.1 TOM'S STEP-BY-STEP PLAN

Ultimate goal: to sleep on my own in my own room all night, every night for a week.

Helpful thought:

Ultimate reward: have four friends over for a sleepover.

Step 4: to sleep in my room alone for two nights in a row.

Helpful thought:

Reward: a trip to the cinema.

Step 3: to sleep in my room alone for one night.

Helpful thought:

Reward: Dad will play a board game with me.

Step 2: to sleep in my room all night with my cousin staying over with me.

Helpful thought:

Reward: a slap-up breakfast in the morning.

Step 1: to sleep in my room all night with Dad in the same room on the camp bed.

Helpful thought: I won't be on my own so I'm sure I'll be fine.

Reward: praise from Mum and Dad.

One thing to remember in setting up a step-by-step plan is that your child cannot make him- or herself actually fall asleep at a particular time. A step like 'be asleep within ten minutes' is guaranteed to fail and is simply going to put more pressure on your child (making it harder for him or her to drop off to sleep). Your child can, however, learn to be comfortable in his or her room alone and learn to settle down to sleep. Some children take longer than others to settle down, and it can become very boring for them lying in their bed not being able to fall asleep. Are there gentle activities that you would be happy for your child to do as he or she calms down for sleep, such as reading or listening to book tapes? Your child may also be reluctant to take the step of being alone in the bedroom. For this reason if your child is not sleeping in his or her own room we recommend getting him or her back in there and getting used to that environment again straight away. Using your step-by-step plan you can then move yourself away from your child, rather than vice versa. So, for example, rather than gradually moving your child out of your room, start with you in your child's room, too, and gradually move yourself away night by night (by sleeping in the room one night, then the following night you would move your bed/mattress nearer to the door. The next night you would be outside the room but not far away, and so on). Similarly, rather than your child coming to check up on you, let your child know that you will check up on him or her every five minutes. Gradually lengthen the period between visits as your child progresses.

Night-time can be a time when children feel particularly vulnerable, but if your child's fear of being alone is not specific to night-time you will need to build early steps in to your plan which allow him or her to get used to being alone in his or her room during the daytime. The essential thing to remember is that each step is taking you forward. Once your child can tolerate the step that you are working on, then move forward.

Worry at bedtime

Most nights it takes us all a little while to fall off to sleep and this is a time when worries that have arisen during the day can pop into our heads and make it harder for us to get to sleep. Or your child may have specific worries that relate to bedtime. For example, some children worry that they will be the last to fall asleep and the only one awake if something were to happen.

If your child is worrying excessively at bedtime, the strategies described in Chapter 11 can be applied. In particular you will find it useful to set a 'worry time' that takes place at another time of day. If your child mentions worries at bedtime, allow these to be added to the worry list and agree to discuss them at the next 'worry time' but don't get drawn into a discussion when your child mentions them. Help your child to come up with ways of relaxing and focusing his or her mind on other things at bedtime. Some people find word-based activities helpful (such as counting activities), others find visual activities more helpful (such as imagining a waterfall flowing). Try out different things and keep track of what works best for your child. Some additional relaxation exercises are also given in Chapter 19.

Other sleep-related problems

Nightmares

As well as being very common, nightmares can also be extremely frightening. Children may wake up in the night and feel too frightened to go back to sleep in case they get the nightmare again. At these times children should be offered comfort and returned to their own beds. Nightmares can relate to something frightening that the child has heard or experienced during the day. It is important to give your child an opportunity, during the daytime, to tell you about the nightmare so that you can help them overcome any fears or worries that appear to have been a trigger using the general principles used in this book.

Night terrors

Typically, night terrors occur within the first hours of falling asleep, when your child is in a deep sleep. The child appears to wake up suddenly (although is actually asleep) and looks terrified. He or she may be screaming, sweating and in a confused state, and have a rapid heart beat. This can last varying amounts of time (such as five to 20 minutes). This is not related to a nightmare, and in the morning your child will generally not remember what happened. Night terrors can occur in people of any age, but are most common in children aged five to 12 years. Although night terrors can be frightening for parents it is important to remember that they are not dangerous.

THE FOLLOWING TIPS MAY HELP REDUCE THE ONSET OF NIGHT TERRORS

1 Make sure your child is not overtired at bedtime. Move bedtime earlier if necessary.

2 Change the pattern of your child's sleep cycle. Try waking up your child soon after he or she has gone to sleep (for example, within an hour) then letting him or her go back to sleep.

3 Check with your general practitioner if your child is on any medication that may be linked to night terrors.

4 Identify and work with your child to resolve any stress that your child is experiencing during the day.

DURING A NIGHT TERROR

1 Don't try to wake your child.

2 Sit with your child and do what you can to make him or her feel comfortable until it passes.

3 If your child is comfortable with this at the time, give him or her a gentle hug.

4 Stay calm. Don't try to reason with your child; just wait for the terror to pass.

Sleepwalking

Similar to a night terror, sleepwalking happens when your child is in a deep sleep and he or she will not remember it in the morning. Similar advice applies: don't try to wake your child, simply quietly steer him or her back to bed. If your child sleepwalks you need to consider whether your house is safe for night-time wanderings. You may need to put a stair gate at the top of the stairs to stop your child falling. Also, be sure to close windows and put away any potentially dangerous objects (or things that could be tripped over) before going to bed.

Bedwetting

In children under the age of six years bedwetting is not unusual. In fact it has been argued that for boys bedwetting is not uncommon and should not necessarily be considered a 'problem' under the age of eight years. If your child is below this age you may nonetheless find it helpful to take practical steps – for example, restricting drinks before bedtime, making sure your child visits the toilet before bed and, perhaps also, waking him or her at your bedtime to visit the toilet again. Children who feel more anxious are more likely to wet the bed than less anxious children so you also need to be using Part Two of this book to overcome any daytime worries that your child is experiencing. You also need to work hard to make sure that the bedwetting does not become a source of anxiety in itself. In order to do this it is important not to punish your child when he or she wets the bed. It will be difficult, but remain calm and try not to show your child your frustration. Instead be very matter of fact about the situation, change the bed and settle your child back to sleep quickly with little fuss. On the other hand, make sure you give your child a lot of praise every time he or she makes it through a night without wetting.

If these steps have not been sufficient and your child is wetting the bed frequently (such as three times a week or more), your general practitioner may be able to refer your child to an enuresis (bedwetting) clinic. In these clinics alarms are often used which identify when your child is beginning to wet the bed. This then wakes your child (and you) so that your child can go to the toilet to finish urinating, the bed can be changed and the alarm reset. For the alarm to work you will have to be prepared to be getting up in the night to go through this procedure, but for the majority of children this works well and quickly.

SLEEP PROBLEMS: KEY POINTS

- Take practical steps to create a good sleeping environment for your child.

- Follow the steps in Part Two, starting with identifying exactly what it is about sleep that your child fears.

- Draw up a step-by-step plan with your child with concrete rewards.

- Make time to discuss night-time worries during the day.

17

Overcoming difficult behavior

Fears and worries can be quite overwhelming for children and young people. Some children will become very tearful in response to them, whereas others will show their reaction with a seemingly angry outburst or tantrum. Both responses reflect the difficulty the child is having keeping control of his or her emotions in the face of anxiety. When children have an outburst like this it can present a real dilemma for parents. On the one hand the parent feels concerned about what has upset the child in this way. On the other hand the child's behavior seems naughty or defiant. In order to manage this behavior it will be necessary to get a good understanding of what has caused this reaction in your child and to overcome the anxiety (using the principles in Part Two) but *you cannot attempt the strategies described in Part Two while your child is in the midst of a tantrum.*

Your child also needs to learn that a behavioral outburst is not an acceptable way of expressing emotions. This chapter will give an overview of useful strategies that can be applied when an outburst occurs. Once things have calmed down you must then, however, take the opportunity to return to Part Two to identify and overcome any fears or worries that may have provoked this difficult behavior.

Attention and praise

We talked before about how positive behaviors can be built up by being on the lookout for them and giving them a lot of attention and praise. Often simply removing attention from negative behaviors and giving attention to other behaviors can make a big difference to how your child behaves. Changing where we focus our attention takes work, as much of the time we can't help noticing the 'bad' things while the 'good' things don't get noticed or are taken for granted. Think about a behavior that you want your child to stop. Now think about what you would like your child to be doing instead. This is what you need to be focusing your attention on.

When behaviors can't be ignored

Sometimes your child may act in a way that cannot be ignored. This is the case when, as a result of his or her behavior, someone could get hurt – for example, if your child becomes aggressive. It is essential that your child learns that this is both an inappropriate and an unhelpful way to solve problems. The following strategies are reserved only for behaviors that are completely unacceptable and should be used sparingly. If the behavior is simply annoying but not actually hurting anyone, then stick with the strategy of ignoring the annoying behavior and being on the lookout for and praising the positive alternative. All of these strategies should also be carried out in as calm and controlled a manner as you can muster. What you are teaching your child here is self-control, so take the opportunity to set a good example of this to your child.

Time out

Time out is based on the principle that children respond to attention. Calmly removing a child from a situation completely, to a situation where there is no attention available, can be a powerful learning experience. Through time out children can learn (i) that certain behaviors are not tolerated by other people; and (ii) that by leaving the situation it can be easier to calm down, allowing us to sort problems out more effectively. Time out can be done by either putting your child in a different room or (for younger children) moving him or her to a different part of the room and withdrawing your attention. Before using time out the situations in which you will be using it need to be clear to your child. The most common reason that time out doesn't work is that it gets overused (children get put in time out for any little thing) and it therefore becomes meaningless or even a game. Write a (short!) list of the behaviors that will lead to time out and put it where it can be clearly seen (such as on the fridge). Your child also needs to know how long the time out will last. A general rule of thumb is one minute for each year of your child's life. Time out should not go on indefinitely – your child needs to know how long he or she has to compose him- or herself and needs to be able to remember why it was started in the first place. Your child also needs to know what behavior you would like to see at the end of the time out. If your child is not behaving in this way by the end of time out, rather than extend the length of the time out we would recommend you then bring in another strategy (such as loss of privileges, see below). The reason for this is that your child could, otherwise, end up being in time out for much longer than he or she can tolerate (reducing the chances of good behavior at the end of it) and not remembering why he or she was there in the first place! Finally, when the time out is over, don't hold a grudge. In fact, when you do see the behavior that you want at the end of the time out this should be praised, as your child has managed to take control of his or her emotions.

BOX 17.1 TIME OUT

To recap, do not use time out until you have established:

• In exactly which situations you will be using it.

• How long time out will last.

• What you would like your child to be doing by the end of time out.

Actions and consequences

Children need to learn that their actions have consequences. Sometimes aggressive behavior has 'natural consequences'. For example, if your child wrecks his or her bedroom he or she will have to live in a messy bedroom until he or she clears it up. This may be more difficult for you than for your child, but do let him or her experience the consequence of his or her behavior, rather than trying to protect him or her (or you) from it.

You can also create particular consequences for your child's actions. One way of doing this is by removing privileges or special items. To have an impact on your child you need to be removing meaningful items or privileges and you need to be removing them as an immediate consequence of your child's action. What you select will depend on your child's age and interests – for example, removing the games console from the bedroom for a day, cutting late nights out for a week.

It is important to remember, however, that the best strategy is always to find ways to encourage your child to behave in a positive way (for example, giving praise or rewards whenever your child shows self-control in the face of emotion). Time out and removing privileges should be used sparingly.

A final word about consistency

Your child is going to find it easier to learn what kinds of behaviors are acceptable if you are consistent in how you respond. If your child has two parents or caregivers, then sit down with the other adult and generate a list of behaviors that are causing problems for your child and how you are going to manage them. Your child is going to learn about how to behave in the face of anxiety most effectively if you are both responding in the same way.

OVERCOMING DIFFICULT BEHAVIOR: KEY POINTS

• Make sure you know how you would like your child to behave (not just how you don't want him or her to behave), and pay attention to that.

• Set a good example to your child of how you keep control of your emotions.

• Limit use of the following strategies to aggressive behavior:

(i) Time out

(ii) Clear and immediate consequences

• Be consistent in how you respond to your child's behavior.

18

School refusal

You may have noticed that your child gets nervous about going to school. This is often the case for anxious children, who can have problems attending school.

Why do children find going to school hard?

If children interpret school-related activities as potentially threatening it is understandable that they attempt to avoid these situations. There are various demands involved in going to school that may present your child with a challenge. This could be because he or she finds it difficult to separate from you or another caregiver, or because he or she will have to answer questions in class, take tests, work in small groups, mix with other children at playtime or cope with what other children might say to him or her. It is also possible that he or she is anxious about going to school because he or she is being bullied, and we will talk about how to tackle this later.

What should you do if your child refuses to go to school?

The first thing you need to do if your child refuses to go to school or gets very anxious or nervous before school is to find out what it is about school that is making him or her nervous. Just as you have practised in relation to other fears and worries, the first step is to ask your child simple questions to try to get a good understanding of the fear. Examples include 'What worries you about going to school?', 'What do you think will happen if you do go to school' or even 'What is the worst thing that might happen if you do go to school?' Your child may be reluctant to tell you why he or she is worried. Children are often concerned that their parent will storm into school to sort out the problem, making the child feel even more the centre of attention or making others think they are a 'tell-tale'. Persistence and trying different ways to ask your child about his or her fears and worries will probably be necessary, as will giving your child an assurance that you won't take any action without his or her agreement.

If you are really unable to get information from your child about the source of the worries, it will be necessary to make an opportunity to talk with your child's teacher or someone else who knows your child well. It is important to be open with your child that you are doing this, but also to let him or her know that you are doing this as discreetly as possible so that it does not lead to increased anxiety about making the bullies target him or her even more.

Once you have established what your child fears or is worried about, you need to make a plan of action in discussion with him or her. If your child has identified a particular problem that you both feel needs sorting out, use the strategies outlined in Chapter 10 to generate ways to solve the problem and evaluate them.

If you discover that there is no particular problem at school but your child feels anxious about certain school activities or situations, such as answering questions in class or doing PE, take the opportunity to investigate and test this fear, and devise a step plan with him or her to face the particular fear just as Jenny and her mother did (see Chapter 9).

Getting support from your child's school

You may be concerned that your child's school is not going to look kindly on the fact that your child has been missing school. In today's climate there is so much press attention on parents being prosecuted for their children's failure to attend school that parents can feel persecuted and as if they and the school are on opposing sides. It is certainly the case that schools do worry about children who are not in school and sometimes involve an education welfare officer who is responsible for monitoring and encouraging a child's attendance. Legally, your child should be in school full-time. However, being anxious about school is an understandable reason why your child might be missing school. It is our experience that schools are generally very understanding and helpful if they can see that you are trying to get your child back into school, and they will appreciate your efforts to work with them to get your child back into school full-time.

Schools and education welfare services are very familiar with the principle of children taking a step-by-step approach to returning to school. This must, of course, be negotiated with the school from the start, so you will need to arrange a meeting with your child's teacher, head teacher or head of year, and anyone else involved in monitoring and supporting your child's attendance. At this meeting discuss the possibility of working out a step-by-step plan with the school. If your child is currently not attending school, this may involve your child gradually building up the amount of time that he or she spends at school. It is important not to take for granted how hard this may be for your child, so concrete rewards should be worked out in advance and given as quickly as possible after your child meets the goal.

It is also useful to establish whether there is somewhere that your child can go to calm down and where he or she feels a bit safer so that he or she can withdraw from stress without having actually to leave the school grounds. A resource unit is an excellent place to go to, but not all schools have them. If your child's school doesn't have one, ask the teacher where else might be a good place for your child to go. It could simply be the head of year's office or the main office. Having a named person to go to if your child feels anxious can also be important. It will also be necessary to negotiate how your child gets access to this place or person – for example, if he or she feels overwhelmed during a lesson and unable to express his or her concerns to the teacher or in front of the class. Schools are sometimes able to give a child a card that he or she can present to the teacher, rather than having to speak up, which will allow him or her time out to calm down at times of high anxiety.

Another good system is the use of buddies, where the school identifies an older pupil who your child can go to for support if he or she needs it, or perhaps meet up with each day to discuss how he or she is getting on.

The central message behind all of this is that the aim should be gradually to build up your child's attendance with as many systems in place as possible to help him or her be comfortable staying in school for as long as has been set out in the step-by-step plan. You will achieve this most successfully if you work as a team with your child's school.

Should I move my child to a different school?

Often parents who come to our clinic with children who are not attending school ask whether changing schools would be a good idea. Their child is often very keen to move schools as he or she feels it will solve all the problems. Children are likely to believe that they won't feel anxious at a new school and that they will make lots of friends. Unfortunately, changing schools rarely leads a child to becoming less anxious and usually the same problems occur, perhaps after a short 'honeymoon' period at the new school, when everything goes well. As we have said, children who are highly anxious often find attending school hard because they have to separate from you or another carer, answer questions in class, take tests, do work in small groups, mix with other children at playtime or cope with what other children might say to them. They will still have to do all these things in a new school.

BOX 18.1 HOW TO WORK AS A TEAM WITH YOUR CHILD'S SCHOOL

1 Arrange to speak to your child's teacher or head of year as soon as you notice that your child is regularly missing days at school.

2 Explain why you think your child is anxious about attending school and also ask for the teacher's opinion.

3 Raise any problems that your child has talked to you about at school, such as bullying, so that the school can also start to deal with these.

4 Make a step-by-step plan to help your child get back into school. Do this with both your child and the teacher, as they might also have some good ideas.

5 Talk about the possibility of having a safe place or a teacher for your child to go to, or a buddy.

6 Meet regularly with your child's teacher to review progress and iron out any problems with the step-by-step plan.

7 Be positive about your child's school even if you don't think it has handled the situation very well. If you moan about your child's school, your child is even less likely to go back.

8 Be clear with your child that he or she has to go to school despite the anxieties. Not only does this give the message that avoiding the situation is not an option but it also shows the school that you are serious about getting your child back to school.

On the other hand, if your child's fears and worries about school relate to particular children being nasty to him or her, or feeling that he or she does not have many friends, you may feel that moving school is a logical thing to do. However, even in this situation, a school move may not solve all your child's problems. He or she may find initially at this new school that everyone is nice to him or her and he or she may make some new friends, but if the child found making friends hard before, he or she may well find it hard again. Similarly, if children have been nasty to him or her before, there is a good chance that there will be some children who can be unpleasant at the new school. If your child has poor social skills this might make him or her more of a target for these children. What your child really needs to do is to learn how to make good friends and to deal with other children saying nasty things, together with support from the school.

There are occasionally times when moving schools might help to resolve your child's problems. If, for example, your child has some significant learning problems that can't be sufficiently supported in the current school, a school move might be a sensible option. However, this should be considered only after discussion with your child's teachers to see if there is anything that can be done to support your child better at the current school.

Changing schools is also very unsettling for any child as he or she has to get used to new teachers, new children and a new school layout, and this can cause additional anxiety initially. If you are considering moving your child to a new school, you should think about this very carefully and talk to your child's teacher, who might also be able to give you some good advice.

What about home tuition?

Some children find going to school so hard that they just want to stay at home. They do not want to change schools, as they know that going to another school will also make them feel nervous. Parents sometimes feel that it would be better to educate their child at home, as school is just too distressing for them. Lots of children, and parents, mention home tuition to us at our clinic, and want to know whether this is an option for them. Home tuition is designed for children who cannot go to school. Usually, this is because a child is physically ill – for example, not being able to walk due to a debilitating illness, or undergoing treatment for an illness such as cancer. For these children, school is not always an option. Occasionally, children with a problem that is not physical, such as anxiety or depression, also receive home tuition because it is apparent that their anxiety or depression is so severe at that time that they are not able to go to school. However, this situation is rare and in such a case home tuition is available only for a short period of time and for insufficient hours to cover everything that your child would be learning at school. Our concern for children who are being taught at home is that this is unlikely to make a child's anxiety any better; in fact it may well make it worse. In Chapter 4 we discussed the maintaining role of avoidance in anxiety. Home tuition in effect allows a child to avoid almost all anxiety-provoking situations, as he or she does not need to even leave the house! He or she also misses out on seeing friends. It is much better to try to devise a step-by-step plan to get your child back into school gradually than to allow him or her to stay at home all the time. If your child's anxiety about school is very high, then this plan needs to be very gradual. Very occasionally, home tuition is used as part of a step-by-step plan for highly anxious children. Having home tuition several hours a week might form part of the first few steps of a plan. The next steps would involve either going to school part-time or having home tuition within the school grounds, to help your child to get used to the school environment again. However, in this case your child must be clear that home tuition is part of a short-term, time-limited plan.

What about bullying?

Bullying is something that needs to be tackled. It can involve name-calling, other unpleasant remarks or physical aggression, such as pushing or – more seriously – hitting or fighting. All schools are required to have an anti-bullying policy. This is basically a guide to how they will manage any incidents of bullying within the school. If your child is being bullied, it is important that you talk to the school so that it can deal with it in accordance with its policy. It is important that your child feels that he or she has some control over what happens as a result of the bullying. Your child should be included in open discussions about how bullying will be handled and he or she must have the opportunity to discuss any concerns that he or she has about this so that measures can be taken to resolve these issues.

The first step is that the school is put in a position in which it can look after and take responsibility for your child's best interests. There should be a clear message to your child that bullying is not acceptable and that definite action needs to be taken. In addition, your child will benefit from making a clear plan of how he or she should respond to any further bullying incidents. Use the problem-solving strategies described in Chapter 10 to help your child to work out different ways of responding to bullying situations and evaluate which would be the most effective for him or her.

SCHOOL REFUSAL: KEY POINTS

• Try to find out why your child is refusing to go to school by speaking to him or her and key school personnel.

• Work as a team with your child's school.

• Devise a step plan to help your child get back into school.

- Make sure your child's school tackles any bullying that he or she reports.

- Work with your child to develop solutions to problem situations.

19

Relaxation

In Part One we talked about the physical symptoms of anxiety that your child is likely to experience. These included tummy aches, breathing difficulties and muscle tension.

Who should learn relaxation techniques?

In our clinic, we do not generally tackle these unpleasant physical symptoms of anxiety in their own right, as we tend to find that reducing fear by changing how an anxious child thinks and how he or she behaves has a knock-on effect on these unpleasant sensations. Sometimes, however, the physical symptoms that a child experiences cause a great deal of distress and the child needs to learn (i) that these physical symptoms are not harmful; and (ii) that he or she can take control of them. The strategies throughout Part Two will help you to find ways with your child to investigate the view that these symptoms are harmful – for example, by looking into the evidence and carrying out experiments. This chapter describes additional ways in which your child can learn to take control of these physical symptoms.

What do relaxation techniques do?

Relaxation techniques do three things. The first is they reduce muscle tension. We know that when people become anxious their muscles become tight. As we described in Part One, this indicates that your child's body is preparing to take action because the brain has given the body the message that there is danger around. Muscle tension is an unpleasant feeling and may result in headaches or other physical signs of anxiety. The second thing that relaxation techniques do is to help us control our breathing. When we are anxious, we breathe more quickly and less deeply, so less oxygen enters our bodies. This leads to various physical sensations: your child may feel like he or she cannot breathe or has butterflies in his or her stomach. The third role of relaxation is to give your child a sense of control over fears or worries by taking action.

How does your child learn to relax?

Your child is likely to find it difficult to relax, particularly if he or she is feeling anxious. To achieve relaxation, therefore, can take a lot of practice. We recommend that children practise the strategies described in this chapter every day at the same time, until they get really good at them. Your child will need your help to do them initially, and so it is best if you do them together. Often a good time to practise relaxation techniques is before bed, as part of your child's bedtime routine. This may have the added bonus of helping him or her to sleep better!

Different types of relaxation techniques

Most relaxation techniques aim to reduce muscle tension, control breathing or create calming mental imagery. There are a number of different ways you can do this and so a number of different relaxation strategies are available. You may well have seen relaxation tapes for sale or read about how to relax in the newspaper or on the Internet. Some relaxation techniques are very quick and take only a few minutes, whereas others take up to half an hour to complete. In principle, it is better to take longer to relax as it is likely to work better, particularly to start with. As your child gets more skilled at relaxing, he or she can cut down the amount of time taken doing the relaxation strategies.

Here we will describe three different relaxation techniques that can be used independently or in combination.

Muscle tension and relaxation

Progressive muscle relaxation teaches your child to relax his or her muscles, focusing on one group of muscles at a time. To do these exercises, your child needs to find somewhere comfortable and quiet to sit or lie down. As we have said, it is probably best if you do the exercises together at least at first. Try to find a time when neither of you will be disturbed.

This process involves getting your child to tense and relax all of the muscle groups one after the other. You may be wondering why we are getting your child to tense muscles when this is the very thing we are trying to reduce! Relaxing muscles is a very abstract concept and not very easy to do. It is much easier to get children to first tense muscles, then relax them, as they can then clearly see the difference between their muscles when they are tense and tight and when they are relaxed. As you go though the exercises with your child, you can ask them at different points, 'Does that feel tight?', 'Does that muscle feel different now you have relaxed it?', 'Can you notice the difference?' He or she should tense their muscles so that they feel tight but are not actually painful. For each muscle group, he or she should tense the muscle group for three seconds (count to three slowly) and then relax the muscles for three seconds (count to three slowly) using the guidelines on the next page. The relaxing part is most important, so he or she can relax the muscles for a little longer if they like.

These exercises should take about five to ten minutes. If you find your child is doing them more quickly, slow things down by having a bigger gap between each exercise, and by doing more than three seconds relaxing after each muscle group has been tightened.

Breathing

Your child needs to learn to breathe both slowly and deeply in order to relax properly. If his or her breathing is very shallow, this is likely to make him or her feel more anxious. First of all, show your child how to breathe in through the nose and out through the mouth. Second, your child should count to three slowly in the head when breathing in, and count to four slowly when breathing out. So he or she should breathe out for a bit longer than breathing in. By counting, your child is automatically slowing down his or her breathing, which we know can get quicker when he or she is anxious. Finally, you need to make sure your child is breathing nice and deeply. You can tell if he or she is by seeing if the chest moves up and down as he or she breathes in and out. If it does, he or she is breathing quite deeply, but encourage him or her to breathe even more deeply by taking deep breaths in and out. If the chest hardly moves, then breathing is quite shallow and he or she needs to work on breathing more deeply, as this will get more oxygen into the body.

When your child has practised this type of breathing he or she can use it between tensing and relaxing exercises, rather than doing it afterwards. For example, he or she can tense and relax the hands, then do some slow deep breathing, before tensing and relaxing the arms, and so on. When your child gets really good at slow breathing, he or she could say 'relax' to him- or herself while breathing out, rather than counting, so that he or she can begin to associate the word 'relax' with this relaxed state.

BOX 19.1 MUSCLE RELAXATION

Hands: clench each fist (one at a time) for three seconds and then relax each hand for three seconds.

Arms: bend each elbow so the wrist nearly touches the shoulder (one at a time) and hold for three seconds, then relax each arm for a further three seconds.

Legs: point the toes and straighten the leg, pushing the knee down, so both the calf and thigh muscles tighten for three seconds, then relax this leg for three seconds. Repeat with the other leg.

Bottom: squeeze the bottom as if trying to lift it off the bed or chair for three seconds, then relax it for three seconds.

Stomach: pull the stomach in and hold for three seconds, then relax it for three seconds.

Chest: stick the chest out like a bodybuilder and take a deep breath in, hold it for three seconds then relax for a further three seconds.

Shoulders and neck: pull the shoulders up to the ears (or as close as they can get), and hold for three seconds, then relax for a further three seconds.

Mouth: clench the teeth and do a big, wide smile and hold for three seconds, then relax the mouth completely for three seconds.

Eyes: scrunch up the eyes so that they are tightly shut for three seconds, then relax the eyes, but keep them shut for at least three seconds.

Forehead: put a hand on the head to make sure it does not move! Raise the eyes to look at the ceiling so that the forehead becomes wrinkled. Hold for three seconds and relax for three seconds.

Slow, deep breathing is also a great thing to do if your child feels anxious when out and does not want to do the tensing and relaxing exercises in front of others. People rarely notice how other people breathe, so he or she could do this without drawing any attention to him- or herself.

Imagery

Another powerful way to relax is using mental imagery techniques – in other words helping your child to create a relaxing scene in his or her mind. There are lots of different techniques you can use; some take a few minutes, some a lot longer. This is the area where you and your child can be most creative.

One of the best strategies is to get your child to close his or her eyes and think of a favourite place, a place that makes him or her feel calm, happy and relaxed. This works best if the child chooses the place that he or she wants to 'go' to for him- or herself. It could be a favourite beach from a holiday, the football stadium of a favourite team, his or her bedroom or an imaginary place. Your job is to act as the guide by asking questions to help him or her to recreate the sights, sounds and smells of that place. Encourage your child to tell you about these things in as much detail as possible. For example, can he or she hear the sea, or the birds, or even the wind, can he or she smell the salt of the sea? Can he or she hear the crowd cheering, music playing or smell the hot dogs? Allow your child to enjoy this image for as long as is comfortable before he or she gently opens his or her eyes while hanging on to that relaxed sensation.

When should my child use these exercises?

As we have said, relaxation techniques are a skill that needs to be learned and practised over and over again. Your child is unlikely to find them easy. Practise the strategies that we have outlined above with your child every day until you notice that he or she is able to relax more and more easily.

It is a good idea to continue doing them every day even when he or she has got really good at them, so that this skill is not lost. Your child will then find

244

it easier to use these techniques at times when he or she actually feels anxious – for example, in the morning before an important test.

A word of warning

Some children find relaxation exercises quite boring and they are not terribly keen to do them. If this is how your child responds to your attempts to help him or her relax, he or she will not be the only one! For this reason, you need to try to make these exercises as fun as possible. For example, the difference between tension and relaxation can be demonstrated by pretending to be two different characters, one who is very stiff and another who is very floppy. This particularly helps younger children who find relaxation exercises difficult to grasp if they are very abstract. To help engage your child, try to think about two characters that your child is interested in: one who is very stiff and another who is very floppy. Some examples are given below.

BOX 19.2

Stiff examples	Floppy examples
A robot	A rag doll
A breadstick	A jelly
A cat about to pounce	A cat asleep on the bed

For the breathing exercises try challenging your child to breathe as quietly as he or she possibly can – this breathing is likely to be slow and deep, just what you are trying to encourage. Finally, for mental imagery the key thing is that the scene that your child is creating is one that he or she has chosen. You may think it is a very strange choice if the aim is to relax but the image chosen is lively (such as a noisy football stadium), but the important thing is that it is your child's choice.

Everyday activities

If, however, despite valiant attempts to interest your child in relaxation exercises he or she is still not interested, all is not lost because some everyday activities can be an extremely effective form of relaxation.

True relaxation describes a state in which we are not thinking about what has happened in the past or is going to happen in the future, but we are in a state of calm in the here and now. Simply engaging in an activity that is enjoyable and uses his or her full concentration will help your child to relax. This could be anything like watching an engrossing film, doing sports, cooking or doing crafts. Exercise can be a particularly good form of relaxation. It can also help to lift people's mood and improve sleep. Exercise can be something as simple as walking the dog or walking down to the local shops. The most important thing is that the activity must be something your child really enjoys and is not a source of additional anxiety. Once you have identified what sort of activities allow your child to relax, make sure you build them into their weekly routine so that your child gets a regular break from fears and worries.

RELAXATION: KEY POINTS

• Relaxation techniques are particularly good for children who experience lots of physical symptoms of anxiety.

• Find ways of explaining relaxation exercises that fit with your child's interests.

• Get your child to practise the relaxation exercises regularly.

• Build enjoyable activities and exercise into your child's routine.

Appendix 1

Useful resources

Further reading

Books for parents

Helping Your Anxious Child, Ron Rapee, Sue Spence, Vanessa Cobham and Anne Wignall, New Harbinger Publications (2000). A book for parents using cognitive and behavioral principles.

What to Do When Your Child Has Obsessive-Compulsive Disorder: Strategies and Solutions, Aureen Pinto Wagner, Lighthouse Press (2004). Strategies for parents to minimize the impact of OCD on your child and family.

Helping Your Child with Selective Mutism, Angela McHolm, Charles Cunningham and Melanie Vanier, New Harbinger Publications (2005). A book for parents using cognitive and behavioral principles.

Tantrums and Tempers, John Pearce, Thorsons Publishing Group (1989). Advice for parents on managing young children's challenging behavior.

The Incredible Years: Trouble-shooting Guide for Parents of Children Aged 3–8, Carolyn

Webster-Stratton, Umbrella Press (1992). Behavior management advice for parents of children aged three to eight years.

101 Ways to Deal with Bullying: A Guide for Parents. Michele Elliott, Hodder (1997). Advice for parents on how to help their child prevent and overcome bullying.

The Unwritten Rules of Friendship: Simple Strategies to Help Your Child Make Friends, Natalie Madorsky Elman and Eileen Kennedy-Moore, Little Brown and Co. (2000). Advice for parents to help children learn the skills to master social relationships.

The following books are just a selection from the Overcoming series that are suitable for adults.

Overcoming Anxiety, Helen Kennerley, Constable & Robinson Ltd (2009).

Overcoming Social Anxiety and Shyness, Gillian Butler, Constable & Robinson Ltd (2009).

Overcoming Depression, Paul Gilbert, Constable & Robinson Ltd (2009).

Overcoming Low Self-Esteem, Melanie Fennell, Constable & Robinson Ltd (2009).

Books for children

Mr Jelly, Roger Hargreaves, Egmont Books Ltd (2003). For preschool children. A great book giving children the message that if you stop and think, rather than jump to conclusions about a threat, things may not be so scary.

Little Miss Shy, Roger Hargreaves, Egmont Books Ltd (2003). For preschool children. Another great book giving children the message that if you face your fears you can overcome them and may end up enjoying yourself.

I Don't Know Why ... I Guess I'm Shy, Barbara Cain and J.J. Smith-Moore, Magination Press (1999). For children aged four to eight years. A story of how a boy overcomes shyness, with information and tips for parents.

Up and Down the Worry Hill: A Children's Book about Obsessive-Compulsive Disorder and Its Treatment, Aureen Pinto Wagner, Lighthouse Press (2004). Award-winning book for children, describing the nature of OCD and its treatment.

No Worries, Marcia Williams, Walker Books (2000). For children aged four to eight years. A picture story that promotes the idea that it is good to talk about worries.

Think Good – Feel Good: A Cognitive Behaviour Therapy Workbook for Children and Young People, Paul Stallard, John Wiley and Sons Ltd (2002). A practical workbook for children and teenagers (from about six years upwards) using cognitive behavioral principles.

How to Be a Friend: A Guide to Making Friends and Keeping Them, Laurie Krasny Brown and Marc Brown, Little Brown and Co. (1998). A cartoon-based book giving children advice on building friendships and dealing with difficulties with other children.

The Willow Street Kids Beat the Bullies, Michele Elliott, Macmillan Children's Books (1986). One of a series of books aimed at children aged seven to 11 years. About a group of schoolfriends and how they cope, avoid, overcome and recover from bullying.

Wise Guides: Bullying, Michele Elliot, Hodder Children's Books (2005). A user-friendly book for older children and teenagers about how to cope with bullying and seek help. Includes chapters on assertiveness and self-esteem.

Useful contacts

UK

British Association for Behavioural and Cognitive Psychotherapies (BABCP)
The Globe Centre
PO Box 9
Accrington BB5 0XB
Tel.: 01254-875277
Fax: 01254-239114
Website: www.babcp.org.uk
Email: babcp@babcp.com
Lists accredited cognitive therapists.

British Association for Counselling and Psychotherapy
BACP House
15 St John's Business Park
Lutterworth
Leicestershine LE17 4HB
Tel.: 0870-443-5252
Fax: 0870-443-5161
Website: www.bacp.co.uk
Information and list of counsellors and psychotherapists.

The British Psychological Society
St Andrew's House
48 Princess Road East
Leicester LE1 7DR
Tel.: 0116-254-9568
Fax: 0116-247-0787
Website: www.bps.org.uk
Email: enquiry@bps.org.uk
Lists chartered clinical psychologists.

Bullying Online
Website: www.bullying.co.uk

Information and advice for children who are experiencing bullying and for their parents (and for children who are bullying and their parents).

ChildLine
Tel.: 0800-1111
Website: www.childline.org.uk

Free helpline for children and young people.

Disaster Action
PO Box 849
Woking GU21 8WB
Website: www.disasteraction.org.uk

Offers support and information for the bereaved and survivors of major disasters and other events.

National Phobics Society
Zion Community Resource Centre
339 Stretford Road
Hulme
Manchester M15 4ZY
Tel.: 0870-122-2325
Fax: 0161-227-9862
Email: info@phobics-society.org.uk
Website: www.phobics-society.org.uk
Information and resources on all anxiety disorders.

OCD Action
22–24 Highbury Grove
Suite 107
London N5 2EA
Tel.: 0870-360 OCDA (6232)
Fax: 020-7288-0828
Website: www.ocdaction.org.uk
Email: info@ocdaction.org.uk

A charity offering help and support for sufferers (children and adults) of OCD.

Oxford Cognitive Therapy Centre
Psychology Department
Warneford Hospital
Oxford OX3 7JX
Tel.: 01865-223-986
Fax: 01865-226-411

Provides cognitive behavioral treatment for children and adults and training for professionals.

Parentline Plus
Tel.: 0808-800-2222
Website: www.parentlineplus.org.uk

A charity offering support and advice to anyone parenting a child.

The Royal College of Psychiatrists: Child and Adolescent Mental Health
Website: www.rcpsych.ac.uk

Contains downloadable reading materials and tapes for children and adolescents experiencing mental health problems, and their parents and teachers.

Triumph Over Phobia (TOP U.K.)
PO Box 3760
Bath BA2 3WY
Tel.: 0845-600-9601
Website: www.triumphoverphobia.com
Email: info@triumphoverphobia.org.uk

A charity providing information, resources and group treatments for phobias and OCD.

The UK Trauma Group
Website: www.uktrauma.org.uk
Information and list of services.

YoungMinds
48–50 St John Street
London EC1M 4DG
Tel.: 020-7336-8445
Fax: 020-7336-8446
Website: www.youngminds.org.uk
Email: enquiries@youngminds.org.uk

A charity providing information and advice for children and young people experiencing mental health problems and for their parents and teachers.

Youth in Mind
Website: www.youthinmind.co.uk

Information and resources for young people, parents and teachers and information on finding services.

SPECIALIST CHILD ANXIETY CLINICS
Child Anxiety Clinic
and
Child Traumatic Stress Clinic
Michael Rutter Centre
Maudsley Hospital
Denmark Hill
London SE5 8AZ

Tel.: 0203-228-3381
Fax: 0203-228-5011
Accept national referrals for assessment and treatment.

The University of Reading Child Anxiety Research Clinic
Dr Lucy Willetts
School of Psychology
University of Reading
3 Craven Road
Reading
Berkshire RG1 5LF
Accepts referrals from across Berkshire for assessment and treatment.

Europe

European Association for Behavioural and Cognitive Therapies (EABCP)
Website: www.eabct.com.

Provides links to national cognitive therapy organizations in Europe. It lists, for example, the website for the Netherlands Association of Behaviour and Cognitive Therapy (which keeps a register of cognitive therapists): www.vgct.nl.

Australia

FRIENDS for life
Website: www.friendsinfo.net

Information on a school-based prevention and treatment program for anxious children and young people. Includes downloadable materials for school personnel.

Macquarie University Anxiety Research Unit (MUARU)

Ronald M. Rapee, PhD, Director
Macquarie University
Sydney NSW 2109
Tel.: 00-612-02-9850-8711
Fax: 00-612-02-9850-6578
Website: www.psy.mq.edu.au/MUARU/

Information, assessment and treatment for children, adolescents and adults with anxiety disorders.

USA

Academy of Cognitive Therapy

One Belmont Avenue
Suite 700
Bala Cynwyd
Pa 19004-1610
Tel.: 00-1-610-664-1273
Fax: 00-1-610-664-5137
Website: www.academyofct.org
Email: info@academyofct.org

Lists accredited cognitive therapists in the USA and many other countries.

American Psychiatric Association
1000 Wilson Boulevard
Suite 1825
Arlington VA 22209-3901
APA Answer Centre: 1 888 35 PSYCH
Website: www.psych.org
Email: apa@psych.org
From outside the USA and Canada: 00-1-703-907-7300
Provides resources for the public on www.healthymi
nds.org.

American Psychological Society
750 First Street
NE, Washington DC 20002-4242
Tel.: 00-1-800-374-2721 or 00-1-202-336-5500
Website: www.apa.org
Keeps a register of psychologists.

Anxiety Disorders Association of America
Website: www.adaa.org

Information on anxiety disorders, including a focus on children and young people.

The Association for the Advancement of Behavior Therapy
305 Seventh Avenue
16th Floor
New York NY 10001-6008
Tel.: 00-1-212-647-1890
Fax: 00-1-212-647-1865
Website: www.aabt.org

Keeps a directory of cognitive and behavior therapists.

Beck Institute for Cognitive Therapy and Research
One Belmont Avenue
Suite 700
Bala Cynwyd PA 19004-1610
Tel.: 00-1-610-664-3020
Website: www.beckinstitute.org
Information, treatment and training provided.

International Society for Traumatic Stress Studies
ISTSS
60 Revere Drive
Suite 500
Northbrook IL 60062
Tel.: 00-1-847-480-9028
Fax: 00-1-847-480-9282
E-mail: istss@istss.org
Website: www.istss.org/resources/index.htm
*Resources and links relating to stress following a
 traumatic event.*

The Child Anxiety NETWORK
Website: www.childanxiety.net

*Information, resources and list of healthcare providers
specializing in treatment of child anxiety.*

WorryWiseKids.org
Website: www.worrywisekids.org
Information for parents.

Appendix 2

Tables

TABLE 7.1: HELPING MY CHILD WITH UNHELPFUL THOUGHTS			
What is happening?	What is he or she thinking?	Evidence and alternatives	What happened in the end?
	Why are you worried? What do you think will happen? What is it about [this situation] that is making you worried?	What makes you think that [this situation] will happen? Has that ever happened to you before? Have you ever seen that happen to someone else? How likely is it that [this situation] will happen? Can you imagine that anything else could happen? If [this situation] did happen, could there be any other reasons for it? What would you think was happening if someone else was in the same boat? What would [another child] think if they were in this situation? How could you test out this thought?	What did your child think? What did your child do? How did your child feel?

TABLE 8.2: RESPONDING TO MY CHILD'S ANXIOUS BEHAVIOR

Date	Behavior What did my child do?	Response What did I do?	Yes	No	Outcome What happened when I did this?
		Cut out reassurance			
		Asked about anxious thoughts			
		Helped him/her find alternative thoughts			
		Gave clear and specific praise			
		Offered a reward			
		Showed how I managed my own fears about the situation			
		Overcame my worries about him/her in this situation			
		Stood back and allowed him/her to 'have a go'			

TABLE 9.1: HOW ANXIOUS DOES MY CHILD FEEL DOING EACH STEP?	
Steps to include in my child's step-by-step plan	How anxious does my child feel in this situation?

TABLE 9.2: MY CHILD'S STEP-BY-STEP PLAN		
Goal	Helpful thought	Reward
10 (ultimate goal)		
9		
8		
7		
6		
5		
4		
3		
2		
1 (easiest step)		

263

TABLE 10.2: PROBLEM SOLVING

What is the problem?	List all the possible solutions (no matter how weird or wonderful!)	What would happen if I chose this solution? (In the short term? In the long term? To my anxiety in the future?)	Is this plan doable? Yes/No	How good is this plan? Rate 0–10	What happened?

TABLE 12.1: HELPING MYSELF WITH UNHELPFUL THOUGHTS			
What is happening?	What am I thinking?	Evidence and alternatives	What happened in the end?
	Why are you worried? What do you think will happen? What is it about [this fear] that is making you worried?	What makes you think that [this fear] will happen? Has that ever happened to you before? Have you ever seen that happen to someone else? How likely is it that [this fear] will happen? Can you imagine that anything else could happen? If [this fear] did happen, could there be any other reasons for it? What would you think was happening if someone else was in the same boat? What would someone else think if they were in this situation? How could you test this out?	What did you think? What did you do? How did you feel?

A

adolescents,
  see teenagers,
aggression, *221, 222, 223*
American Psychological
Society,
  anxiety and phobias, *5, 6,
  19, 20, 24, 48*
  academic performance,
  21, 23
  avoidance behaviors, *41,
  42, 43, 155, 190*
  coping experiences, *34, 35*
  generalized anxiety, *13, 15,
  51*
  influencing by example,
  30, 31, 32, 43, 54, 96, 152, 153
  influencing by reaction,
  32, 33, 35, 43, 88, 90, 97, 98
  inheritance and genetics,
  27, 28, 30, 54
  recognizing real threats,
  83, 125
  separation anxiety, *9, 15, 20,
  207*
  specific phobias, *9, 10, 12, 20,
  37, 38, 51*
  timing and focus of
  treatment, *49, 51*
  see also controlling
  worry; cycles of
  behavior; helpful and
  unhelpful thoughts;
  identifying the problem;
  parental anxiety; problem
  solving; step-by-step
  plan,
attention and praise, *88, 90,
91, 123, 128, 189, 190, 194, 203, 209, 221*
avoidance behavior, *41, 42, 43,
90, 155, 190*
  see also attention and
  praise,

B

bedwetting, *216, 217*
behavioral difficulties, *219,
221, 222, 223*
breathing, *15, 238, 241, 242, 243*
bullying, *83, 126, 232, 234*
  see also problem solving;
  school and teachers,

C

carers,
  see parental anxiety;
  parenting,
Cognitive Behavioral
Therapy,
  see also attention and
  praise; controlling worry;
  goals; helpful and
  unhelpful thoughts;
  identifying the problem;
  problem solving;
  rewards; step-by-step
  plans,
  focus of treatment, *51*
  how it works, *51*
  timing of treatment, *49, 51*
confidence,
  see attention and praise;
  independence,
controlling worry, *139, 144, 145,*
146
  accepting uncertainty, *146,*
  148
  allocating 'worry time',
  141, 142, 148, 155, 214
  cutting out reassurance,
  79, 82, 83, 142
  distractions, *142, 144, 149, 150,*
  190, 246
  see also helpful and
  unhelpful thoughts;
  identifying the problem;
  problem solving;
  relaxation techniques;
  step-by-step plan,
coping experiences, *34, 35*
creativity in therapy, *57, 72,*
105, 141, 186, 187
cycles of behavior, *21, 23, 37,*
38, 40, 42, 43, 88, 90, 191
  see also avoidance
  behavior; life influences;
  parental anxiety,

D

depression, *23, 24, 233*
distractions from worry, *142,*
144, 149, 150, 190, 246
  see also controlling
  worry; relaxation
  techniques,

E

education,
  see schools and teachers,
encouraging your child,
  see attention and praise;
  independence; rewards,
environmental influences,
30, 31, 32, 33, 34, 35, 43, 88, 90, 96, 97, 98

see also cycles of behavior; parental anxiety,

experiments, *81, 82*

F

fears,
  see anxiety and phobias; attention and praise; controlling worry; goals; helpful and unhelpful thoughts; identifying the problem; problem solving; rewards; step-by-step plan; young children (8 and under),
focusing treatment, *51, 177, 178*
  see also goals,
fun in therapy, *57, 105, 141, 149, 150, 245, 246*

G

genetics, *27, 28, 30*
goals, *112, 115, 117*
  defining, *107, 108, 177, 178*
  focusing therapy, *51*
  helpful thoughts, *112, 115, 121*
  slow progress, *170, 171, 172, 173*
  step-by-step approach, *104, 105, 107, 109, 111, 112, 115*

see also attention and praise; controlling worry; identifying the problem; problem solving; record keeping; rewards,

H

headaches, *6, 238*
heart rate,
  see physical symptoms,
helpful and unhelpful thoughts, *61, 64, 84, 115, 119*
  accepting uncertainty, *146, 148*
  evaluating thoughts, *72, 74, 75, 76, 78, 79*
  open and closed questions, *64, 65*
  parental anxiety, *154, 155, 158, 161*
  part of step-by-step plans, *112, 115, 121*
  teenagers, *201, 203*
  young children (8 and under), *186, 187*
home tuition, *233, 234*

I

identifying the problem,
  coaxing and reaffirming answers, *65, 66, 67, 69*

evaluating thoughts, *72, 74, 75, 76, 78, 79, 81*

open and closed questions, *64, 65*

see also goals; problem solving; step-by-step plan; teenagers; young children (8 and under),

imagery for relaxation, *243, 246*

see also relaxation techniques,

Incredible Years: Trouble-shooting Guide for Parents of Children Aged, *4, 5*

independence, *43, 97, 98, 191, 203*

see also controlling worry; cycles of behavior; reassurance,

inherited anxiety, *27, 28, 30, 54*

L

life influences, *30, 31, 32, 33, 34, 35, 43, 88, 90, 96, 97, 98*

see also parental anxiety,

M

muscle tension, *6, 237, 238, 239, 241*

N

nausea,

see physical symptoms,

nightmares and night terrors, *214, 215, 216*

O

Obsessive Compulsive Disorder, *17, 18, 20*

open and closed questions, *64, 65*

see also identifying the problem,

P

panic disorder, *9, 15, 17, 19, 20*

parental anxiety, *54, 96, 97*

anxious signals, *160, 161*

facing fears, *164, 165, 166*

helpful thinking, *154, 155, 158*

problem solving, *168*

record keeping, *153, 161, 164*

support from others, *160, 168*

parenting, *152, 153, 154, 158, 159, 160*

allowing independence, *97, 98, 191, 203*

coping experiences, *34, 35*

how to approach the program, *55, 57, 58*

influencing by example, *31, 32, 43, 54, 96, 152, 153*

influencing by reaction, *32, 33, 34, 35, 43, 88, 90, 97, 98*

inherited anxiety, *27, 28, 30, 54*

recognizing real threats, *83, 125*

timing of treatment, *49, 51*
see also attention and praise; controlling worry; goals; helpful and unhelpful thoughts; identifying the problem; parental anxiety; problem solving; record keeping; rewards; step-by-step plans,

patterns of behavior,
see cycles of behavior,

phobias,
see anxiety and phobias,

physical symptoms, *5, 6, 13, 15, 17, 40, 41*
see also relaxation techniques planning see step-by-step plans,

Post Traumatic Stress Disorder (PTSD), *19, 20*

praise and attention, *88, 90, 91, 123, 128, 189, 190, 194, 203, 209, 221*

problem solving, *125, 126, 127, 136, 155*

attention and praise, *128, 138*

coaxing solutions, *130, 131, 133, 134, 136*

common problems with the program, *172, 173*

identifying the best solution, *131, 133, 144, 145, 146*

identifying the problem, *128*

recognizing real threats, *83, 125*

teenagers, *203*
see also controlling worry; goals; identifying the problem; parental anxiety; step-by-step plans,

progress reports,
see record keeping,

Q

questioning your child,
see identifying the problem,

R

realistic and unrealistic thoughts,

see helpful and unhelpful thoughts,
reassurance, *42*
   cutting out, *79, 82, 83, 142*
   safety behaviors, *123*
record keeping, *57*
   anxious behavior, *98*
   anxious feelings, *112*
   dealing with slow progress, *170, 171*
   helpful and unhelpful thoughts, *84*
   parental anxiety, *153, 161, 164*
   problem solving, *127, 128, 136*
   step-by-step plan, *115*
   teenagers, *203*
   'worry list', *141, 142, 153*
relaxation techniques, *237, 238, 246*
   breathing, *241, 242, 243*
   making it fun, *245, 246*
   muscle tension, *238, 239, 242*
   using imagery, *243, 246*
rewards, *91, 93*
   concerns about, *93, 94, 96*
   immediate, *92, 93*
   parents and carers, *178, 179*
   part of step-by-step plans, *108, 109, 111, 112, 115*
   teenagers, *203*

young children (8 and under), *189, 190, 191*
see also attention and praise,

S

safety behaviors, *123*
schools and teachers, *12, 13, 15, 17*
   academic performance, *21, 23, 232*
   bullying, *83, 126, 232, 234*
   changing, *229, 230, 232*
   home tuition, *233, 234*
   refusal to attend, *225, 226, 228, 229, 230, 232, 233, 234, 235*
   support from, *58, 123, 226, 228, 229, 230, 234*
   see also attention and praise; controlling worry; cycles of behavior; goals; identifying the problem; problem solving; step-by-step plans,
separation anxiety, *9, 15, 19, 20*
   see also sleeping difficulties,
sleeping difficulties, *13, 15*
   see also controlling worries; helpful and unhelpful thoughts;

problem solving;
relaxation techniques,
bedwetting, *216, 217*
correct environment, *207*
nightmares and night
terrors, *214, 215, 216*
sleepwalking, *216*
step-by-step plan, *209, 211, 212*

social phobias, *12, 13, 19, 20*
step-by-step plans, *104, 105, 107, 112, 115, 117*

common problems, *172, 173*
defining goals, *107, 108, 177, 178*
helpful thoughts, *112, 115, 121*
parental anxiety, *164, 165, 166*
rewards, *108, 109, 111, 112, 115*
set-backs and slow
progress, *123, 170, 171, 172, 173*
sleeping difficulties, *209, 211, 212*
see also attention and
praise; controlling
worries; identifying the
problem; problem
solving; record keeping;
rewards; support for
caregiver; young children
(8 and under),
stomachache,

see physical symptoms,
story telling, *187, 211, 245*
support for caregiver,
help with program, *57, 58, 81, 123, 160, 168, 201*
teachers and school, *226, 228, 229, 230*
sweating,
see physical symptoms,

T

tantrums, *219, 221, 222, 223*
teachers,
see schools and teachers,
teenagers, *197, 198, 199*
allowing control, *201*
helpful thinking, *201, 203*
praise and rewards, *203*
step-by-step plan, *203*
testing out fears, *81, 82*
see also goals,
'time out', *221*
trauma and upheaval, *30, 31, 35, 229, 230, 232*

V

visualization techniques, *243, 246*

W

worries,

see anxiety and phobias;
controlling worries;
goals; helpful and
unhelpful thoughts;
identifying the problem;
problem solving;
step-by-step plan,
'worry scale', *112*
'worry time', *141, 142, 148, 155, 214*

Y
young children (8 and
under), *184, 185*
encouraging
independence, *191*
identifying fears, *186*
praise and rewards, *189,
190, 191, 194*
step-by-step planning,
190, 191, 193
suggesting alternative
thoughts, *186, 187*
testing out ideas, *187, 189*

Books For ALL Kinds of Readers

At ReadHowYouWant we understand that one size does not fit all types of readers. Our innovative, patent pending technology allows us to design new formats to make reading easier and more enjoyable for you. This helps improve your speed of reading and your comprehension. Our EasyRead printed books have been optimized to improve word recognition, ease eye tracking by adjusting word and line spacing as well as minimizing hyphenation. Our EasyRead SuperLarge editions have been developed to make reading easier and more accessible for vision-impaired readers. We offer Braille and DAISY formats of our books and all popular E-Book formats.

We are continually introducing new formats based upon research and reader preferences. Visit our web-site to see all of our formats and learn how you can Personalize our books for yourself or as gifts. Sign up to Become A RHYW Registered Reader.

www.readhowyouwant.com